Faith Under Fire
Through Trials of Abuse

Faith Under Fire

Through Trials of ABUSE

Shelly Bronkema

ISBN: 978-1-7346154-0-1 (Paperback)

Library of Congress Control Number: 9781734615401

Publisher's Cataloging-in-Publication Data

Names: Bronkema, Shelly, author.
Title: Faith under fire through trials of ABUSE / by Shelly Bronkema.
Description: Cadillac, MI: Shelly Bronkema, 2020.
Identifiers: LCCN: 2020908042 | ISBN: 978-1-7346154-0-1
Subjects: LCSH Bronkema, Shelly. | Family violence--Biography. | Abused women--Biography. | Marital violence--United States. | Spousal abuse--United States. | BISAC BIOGRAPHY & AUTOBIOGRAPHY / Personal Memoirs. | BIOGRAPHY & AUTOBIOGRAPHY / Women. | FAMILY & RELATIONSHIPS / Abuse / Domestic Partner Abuse.
Classification: LCC HV6626.2 .B76 2020 | DDC 362.8292--dc23

Edited by: Nic Grogan, Miles to Pages Wordsmithing, milestopages@gmail.com
Cover and interior design: Deb Rozeveld, rozeart30@gmail.com

Printed in the United States of America

Memorial

Written in memory of the women who have died
mercilessly at the hands of an abuser.

May God rest their souls, for their lives were
snuffed out during a moment of horror.

Disclaimer

Neither the publisher nor the author are responsible or liable for any emotional distress, trauma, mental anguish, or medical condition that may occur from reading this book. Each individual is to use their own discretion in deciding whether they should read the story or not. The story is not suitable for children and should be treated as such by the discretion of the parent and/or guardian.

The information in this book is not to be used to diagnose or treat individuals. Each person needs to see their own counselor, psychologist, and doctor for their situation.

All names of people and places used in this book, except that of the author, are fictional to protect the privacy of those mentioned.

The story within these pages is true, and while many of the situations were horrendous and painful to live through, the author has done her best to spare the reader graphic details. In these pages you will find the basic facts of what transpired, but for those who are triggered by certain situations, be forewarned that this book contains mention and descriptions of severe emotional abuse, violence, rape, animal cruelty, and mental manipulation.

You have likely heard the saying, "The eyes are the window to the soul." The Bible speaks of this in **Matthew 6:22-24**. "The eye is the lamp to the body. If your eyes are healthy, your whole body will be full of light. But if your eyes are unhealthy, your whole body will be full of darkness." (NIV).

It is believed that you can find what a person thinks and feels, their goals and desires that are a reflection of their heart, by looking into their eyes. When that light is bright, it offers hope and healing to the hurting. When we see darkness in the eyes, it sometimes exists because someone stole the fire from their lamp, and they can no longer shine. Read on to find out if your eyes reflect a light of joy and zeal to offer hope to others, or if there is a cloud of darkness dimming your light with an unhealthy perspective of what a prosperous relationship looks like.

Table of Contents

Sparks of Discernment

Acknowledgements

I'd like to thank Tom Dettloff, a retired sheriff of Osceola county. Your input and support gave me the reassurance I needed to push forward and see this through! A huge thank you to Michael J. Zannitto Jr., a retired police officer, combat medic and veteran of the Gulf War, and a Board Certified Expert in Traumatic Stress. Your valuable expertise will provide countless individuals with hope and guidance.

My deepest gratitude goes out to every single individual who helped make this book possible. There are too many of you to name, but from the bottom of my heart, I appreciate your contributions and how you have rallied around this project. Thank you for being a part of educating others who are unaware of the effects of emotional abuse, and for helping to create a haven of support, solidarity, and awareness for other victims. God bless you all!

Thank you to my children, who have always been my reason to dig deep and find strength when I thought there was none left.

This book would not exist if it weren't for the actions of my abuser. No, this does not mean that he is deserving of thanks, as will become very apparent in the following pages. It does mean, however, that he has my forgiveness, though he may not deserve it or want it, because he also does not deserve the time and energy it would take to hate him. Despite his best efforts, I heal, I grow, and I thrive. Despite his darkness, I rise.

Prologue

Over the years, I have been blessed to connect with a variety of people through the different career paths I have chosen, from fighting fires to styling hair. One might think that the more heroic profession is firefighting, and it's true, there are plenty of chances to save lives and make an impact. But what many do not immediately see is that there is always occasion for offering a helping hand or a listening ear. Throughout my time as a hairstylist, the Lord has given me ample opportunity to help women who have been in abusive situations. When victims were afraid, they knew they could come in to get pampered and discuss the obstacles they were facing in their relationships.

Many of the stories were the same, with emotional abuse being the emphasis. Physical abuse is well-defined but many people still have questions about emotional abuse.

Is emotional abuse something you leave a relationship over? Can it be just as damaging as physical abuse? Are my kids safe since there are no signs of physical violence?

In *Faith Under Fire Through Trials of Abuse*, I share my personal story of what I experienced with emotional abuse and how the church reacted to my situation. Although leaving a spouse isn't right for everyone, it was something I had to do for my safety.

In the following pages, I have recorded the details of my personal experience in the hopes that others who can relate might take courage and take action, for their own health and safety and that of any family members. I realize that many of you may believe in a higher power other than the one that guided me to safety. I want you to know that I respect your spiritual views, and request that you don't allow your personal beliefs to dictate whether you choose to read or not to read *Faith Under Fire Through Trials of Abuse*. The main subject of the book is how emotional abuse reveals itself. The spiritual aspect in this case was used against me and is a contributor to the emotional abuse I received. There are many valuable examples presented to give you a better understanding of emotional abuse, and my desire is to bring hope and light to that which fear would have us keep in the dark.

I invite you on this difficult but worthwhile journey to uncover the mysteries of emotional abuse and learn how it can affect a person's perspective on life and one's health. Though you may be weary, you are brave and you are strong enough.

ONE

BACKDRAFT OF MEMORIES

The brisk winter of northern Michigan closed in around my hometown. Air moisture was low, and the dry weather made conditions favorable for a structure fire. I made myself available to answer any fire calls that may be dispatched to our station that evening. As paid volunteers, we were not required to spend our time at the firehouse. When we would get a call, those who were readily available would rush to make it in before the truck went out to the fire. I lived the furthest away, and did not want to run the risk of getting snowed in or getting stuck scraping ice off of my car when I could be helping to tame blazing flames or assisting drivers at the scene of an accident. It made more sense to camp out at the fire station so that I would be ready to go, should a call come in.

The firehouse was empty, and as the snow fell outside, I settled in for the wait. Cozy in my oversized sweatshirt, surrounded by quiet rooms and halls, there was just one thing left to do. I looked for the clicker and turned the television on.

The image displayed on the screen showed a ranch-style house marked off with police tape that read, "DO NOT CROSS." I listened intently as the narrator revealed the gruesome details of a mother and her children, murdered at the hands of her husband. The scene left me to wonder, In the days prior to her death, did she have a clue that her life was about to end?

I felt a chill run down my spine and could feel my blood sugar drop. My muscles shook uncontrollably, while my heart raced and teeth chattered. I was experiencing an episode of fight or flight, unsure if I wanted to stick around and continue to watch the narrative, since it so vividly reminded me of my past. The all-too-familiar inner battle began to stir up from my core, but I had been training for this, even when it wasn't a conscious effort. Choosing to stay and fight through the symptoms meant not allowing my abuser to win another round of emotional turmoil.

After I settled on what I was going to do, I grabbed a blanket and curled up on the couch with a sugary cup of hot chocolate. I am tough now, *I told myself.* It's been six long years since I felt that horrific sense of danger from the hands of my ex-husband. Why do I still feel the need to convince myself that my children and I will be safe?

In the hours to follow, the memories of my traumatic past raged through my thoughts like a sudden backdraft in a structure fire.

The Past

I met Jack-- a short, husky, outspoken individual-- at a Christian college in central Florida in 1988. Jack won my heart with his desire to defend my naive tendencies, and a willingness to be my compass when I couldn't tell if people were joking with me or not.

I went to college with intentions to graduate with a major in music, since the best parts of my high school years were spent in band and choir. As I matured, my love for music developed into a passion to play piano and sing. This musical combo brought me joy as I hammered out each note and belted lyrics enthusiastically.

I saw Jack for the first time when he held the front door open to the dormitory. I walked past him to let myself out of the building. I caught his attention and from that point on, he kept me in his sights.

The first few days on campus were spent getting to know each other. During that time Jack expressed his interest in me with jokes, charming gestures, and he even tried to make me jealous, in a somewhat typical, albeit unhealthy manner that too often accompanies the early moments of infatuation and the dating world. But the tables were turned one day when I unintentionally made him jealous during a class visit to Lake Hollingsworth. For the first thirty minutes of the excursion, Jack walked in the park with me, then suddenly darted ahead to join a group of girls from our class. At first I was too caught up with the unfamiliar landscape to notice he was gone. The bald cypress trees exquisitely decorated with Spanish moss, set against the bright blue skies, had my full attention as I soaked in the sunshine. By the time I realized that I had been left behind, he had put quite a bit of distance between us, which left me to myself. There was a catch of fear in my breath until I spotted two guys from my class. I was relieved that they extended an invitation to join them for the remainder of the walk.

When we returned to the entrance of the park we found the class ogling over the large alligator that was kept in a pit below ground level for visitors to view. The rumor was that you wouldn't be eaten by the massive reptile if you threw in coins and made a wish. Jack approached me and watched as I threw coins in with my wish. I was having fun and it had been a good day so far. But then I looked up and saw his face. He had lost his joy somewhere on the trail with all those girls. I could feel his somber disposition as he moved toward me. He spoke with deep, serious tones and made it clear that I would no longer be allowed to hang out with other guys. He paused for a moment to gather his thoughts, then with slowed speech he spoke. "I want you to know that you are now my girlfriend."

I was thrilled Jack wanted to have a relationship with me, but his approach left me confused. It didn't seem right for him to command me to be his girl.

The Chat

In November of that year, my English professor, Miss Prudence, heard of my plans to marry Jack. One day after chapel she invited me into her office to discuss the news that had traveled throughout the entire campus.

I dreaded the talk and expected a lecture about why I should wait to get married. She sat down at her desk, and instead began to discuss some of the challenges I might face in my marriage. Once I realized that she was on my side and just attempting to give me helpful advice, I relaxed and listened intently to her counsel. It was her final thought that stuck with me, and one that I would recall years down the road.

"No matter what struggles you endure in your marriage, be sure to always give Jack a hot meal each night, intimate bedroom time, and respect."

At the time that she shared her perspective, it seemed to be a wise and Biblical ideal. However, looking back, I can now see the destruction that this type of advice can cause.

As Miss Prudence finished imparting her guidance, I felt encouraged. I walked away from our conversation in confidence that I could create a successful marriage.

Over Christmas vacation, Jack and I returned to Michigan. It was during this time that my parents and I met Jack's family. Up until that point, my family had been supportive of my decision to marry, but that changed after our visit. Meeting Jack's mother, Stella, was an interesting experience. I had never met anyone quite like her. While her overall demeanor was prim and proper, the more she talked, the more she revealed her more oppressive qualities. Her loud, boisterous voice dominated any conversation, and she was often rude and prejudiced. During our visit, Stella's monologues were peppered with demeaning remarks toward my family. Jack's father, Wayne, was soft spoken and he quietly went along with whatever Stella said, supporting his wife and her views. After that first meeting of our two families, my parents were hesitant to support the upcoming marriage. They predicted a stormy relationship with Jack and his family, and warned me of their concerns. Their hesitations should have discouraged me from following through with the wedding, but I ignored them.

How could they not see what I saw? Jack adored and respected me, and proved his appreciation for me with many acts of servitude. He was easy to talk to and we were best friends! My heart was torn with their observations, until I realized they weren't with me every day to see how close Jack and I had become. They couldn't see how he protected and helped me. How he loved me in all the intangible ways, like when he would walk me to class, bring me lunch, and help me with my studies.

I especially loved Jack's spontaneity and his funny, boisterous personality. He exposed his biting wit when he would debate scripture with anyone up for the challenge.

On the flip side of all the positives, I took note that he was oppositional, opinionated, and rebellious toward those who had different ideas than he had or those who dared to make him accountable for his actions. Yet, I was intrigued with his intense personality and the way it emanated a mysterious vibe. There was something different about it that appealed to my curiosity.

After the winter months, I left college to prepare for the wedding. During that time, my thoughts were consumed with ways to make a lasting impression on our wedding guests. I wanted them to walk away from the ceremony with hope and encouragement, and I especially wanted this to be the case for those who struggled in their own marriages.

The Closed Heat Vent

I went to stay with Jack's family for a few days as he wrapped up his semester. While his parents and I waited for Jack to arrive home, Stella talked about all the wonderful places they had lived. Their life story sounded as if they had lived from one amazing adventure to another, traveling to see major landmarks and learning the history of each destination. I couldn't imagine what a life of travel would look like since I had only moved a handful of times, all of which were within a thirty mile radius of each other. College was the only time I left the state of Michigan, except for a few visits to Cedar Point, an amusement park in Ohio. Primarily, my life had been about corn, cows, lakes, and trees.

At one point, our conversation turned serious. I felt the scrutiny of Stella's eyes scanning over my body as I sat alone on the couch. She seemed to think it was necessary to grill me about several different aspects of my life, and she did not hide her disdain for my responses. During each awkward pause in our chat, I would listen to the sound of cicada bugs as they hummed outside, along with the deep tones of hornets as they buzzed by. The summer air was warm, yet the living room felt emotionally cold as our conversation became more and more uncomfortable. I squirmed to shift my weight as I tried to cover my bare legs with my arms. I was polite and did not speak out of turn. I answered each question with a soft spirit, until I heard Jack's car pull up in the driveway. Without hesitation, I jumped up from the couch, knocked open the screen door, and dashed out to meet him. I was relieved that my judgment hour with Stella was over.

Jack joined me on the couch after we greeted each other. He placed his arm over my shoulders but the stench from his armpits caused me to curl up my nose and move away from him. I was afraid my gestures would communicate to Stella that I was disinterested in him. I gracefully moved back toward him then signaled for him to keep his arms down.

Jack's voice thundered with excitement as he spoke about his last few months at college. A tinge of guilt coursed through me as I watched his enthusiasm. College life would be different after marriage. I wondered if he had realistically evaluated what his future would look like with me in it.

As the conversation continued, my comfort level increased. I eventually felt much more at ease around Stella and Wayne with Jack in the room, forgetting how awkward the visit had become before he'd arrived.

A cuckoo bird jumped out from the clock at 10 p.m. to signal that it was time to retire for the night. I plopped down on the bed in the guest room and expected to bounce back up. Instead, the bed absorbed my body and beckoned me to lie down. I resisted the urge as I sat cross legged, turning over the events of the day in my mind. Things felt off, and I wasn't able to relax. I took in the clean smells of the room. Quietly, I reflected on the conversation with Stella and Wayne and recalled how I'd felt when she'd scrutinized me. I thought that things had been going well, but it felt as if everything had been turned on me.

My ears suddenly perked up as I began to hear chatter in the basement below me. I looked down at the old heat vent in the floor. The voices crescendoed as they traveled up through the vent system and into the guest room. In spite of the lever on the vent being in the closed position, I heard every word.

I bit my bottom lip and cringed as I recognized Stella's voice. I had been right to feel uncomfortable with her earlier, as the tirade escaping the vent confirmed the judgment I had felt during the awkward conversation before Jack's arrival. For the next two hours, I listened to her yell with disapproval as she demeaned my character. At one point I heard her ask Jack, "Why do you want to marry a girl who has been raised in the sticks of a small hick town?" I realized at that moment that I was not the woman Stella had in mind for her son to marry.

After everyone fell asleep, I called my mother to tell her that I needed to escape the madness that my trip had turned into. I asked for her help but she quickly informed me that it would not be possible for her to drive three hours one way to rescue me. I would have to dig in and stick it out. The days ahead were going to be difficult, as I knew I would experience a crash course in how to cope with my future in-laws. The following morning after breakfast, Stella called everyone together in the living room for a family conference. She was forward and to the point about how she felt about me marrying her son. Her sentiments were summed up in her declaration that she would not be passing on her deceased mother's wedding ring to Jack to give to me. I convinced myself that I was to marry Jack, not Stella. The hurtful words she spoke had no bearing on my decision to marry her son. I quickly learned that I would have to stand up to her attributes of control and rudeness. She did not take well to my boundaries and it created conflict in the days to follow.

TWO

BOUNDARIES FOR BURN CONTROL

a few weeks before the wedding, in the summer of 1989, Stella gave her son an ultimatum. He had the choice to stay home and work while the rest of his family traveled west for vacation, or he could join them if he chose to break off the engagement.

Shortly after their family meeting in which she'd delivered her ultimatum, Stella called to inform me that Jack had experienced an emotional meltdown and would not be available to talk to me for a few weeks. She ended our conversation with a statement that underscored her agenda and earlier ultimatum. "Jack's breakdown has happened because he can't handle the pressures of getting married."

Two weeks passed before I finally heard from Jack. I had been trying to stay positive, keeping myself busy with the wedding plans and work. I couldn't help but worry about him and the confusion he must be feeling. When he finally did call, he was distant and hesitant to emotionally connect with me.

"I don't want to argue with my parents anymore about marriage," Jack declared. "I'm not sure I want to go through with this."

With a soft voice I answered, "Jack, you can't let your parents control you all your life. Don't allow this situation to hold you back from your dreams. Besides, I have already purchased the wedding invitations and we have to go through with it now."

At the time, I felt I was firmly setting boundaries and standing up for our love. Looking back, I can see how using the invitations as a reason to move forward was manipulative and unhealthy. In an attempt to find a path out of the confusion and away from Stella's demeaning ultimatum, I was misguided, a fact only clearly seen in hindsight.

A few days after my phone conversation with Jack, I visited my pastor for premarital counseling. I told him the story of how Stella had pressured Jack not to marry me and how it had caused him to have an emotional breakdown.

The pastor cautioned that there were many red flags warning me of issues I would face in my relationship with my future spouse and in-laws.

My mind was stuck. I couldn't imagine what those issues would look like since I grew up in a happy home with very little conflict after my mother remarried. I resolved that I could overcome any situation that concerned my pastor if I chose to surrender it to the Lord.

The following Sunday after church, a deacon stopped me to

share the statistics of failed marriages in couples who married too young. My heart grew rebellious in response to his opinion, deepening my desire to prove that my marriage would succeed. I liked to watch boxing matches on TV-- I admired the grit and determination of the fighters, and now I felt like I could relate. In my mind's eye, I stood tall in the corner of a boxing ring, confident in my ability to defeat my opponent, in this case, all of the doubts that those around me had in my upcoming nuptials. My pride fueled my desire to fight for what I thought was right for my future, not taking into account that my fans surrounding the ring, and those shouting from the ropes in my corner were only trying to remind me to keep my block up. I mislabeled my pride as surrender to God's will, and after a few weeks Jack warmed back up to the idea of a life together. In spite of all the opposition I encountered, I married Jack anyway.

Sparks of Discernment

Taking Responsibility

At only twenty years old, I believed I knew what a healthy relationship looked like and what it meant to surrender my issues to God. However, when it seemed that God wasn't going to follow through, I took matters into my own hands by doing what I needed to in order to put Jack back on track to fulfill my plans. It was manipulative and unhealthy behavior on my part.

Acknowledging our own negative behavior and improving our conduct are both important aspects of growth. However, our shortcomings never condone maltreatment from another.

Sometimes I hear victims say, "I deserved it, I forgot to do what he said," or "I was late and knew better." These types of statements are the same as saying, "I deserved what was coming to me." No matter what the reason is that we didn't come through in the relationship, it still doesn't condone ill-treatment from others.

Whether we are blinded by our own ideals of what a healthy relationship should look like or we perceive that we deserve punishment, self-abuse or abuse from another is never an acceptable way to handle shortcomings. Instead, we need to do the healthy thing and respect ourselves and expect others to respect us as well.

We all have room to grow. There's an old saying, "God is still working on me." We need to give ourselves grace for not knowing everything about human behavior but still be willing to evaluate, with the wisdom of others we trust, where we are wrong. It is important to take responsibility for our actions with the willingness to improve. Healthy relationships bring quality and joy within the family unit.

Honeymoon

I grabbed Jack's arm as we ran into a shower of rice. I wanted to focus on the joy of the moment and let it carry us into the wedded bliss that I felt we'd worked so hard to reach.

By the time we arrived at our beachfront hotel that overlooked Traverse Bay, the sun had just set, giving us a glorious twilight view. The colors of the sky were picture perfect and the water was like glass. The earth beckoned my bare feet to step outside and walk on the smooth sand by the water's edge.

"Jack, look outside," I said. "It's beautiful! Let's go for a walk."

I glimpsed another pair of newlyweds basking in the beauty of the bay and in each other's love as they wandered along the beach. The groom doted on his bride with loving looks and gentle gestures, fixing her veil here then snapping pictures of her in the late light there. I yearned for that connection and affection in that gorgeous natural setting. Instead, Jack reached up to swiftly remove the bobby pins from my hair, then walked me over to the bedside. Suddenly we were both stricken with sharp stomach pains. Instantly, I knew what I had done wrong.

"Jack, the Holy Spirit is grieving over our decision to marry."

He looked up at me from his hunched over position and answered back, "I don't think God wanted us to marry each other either."

Neither Jack nor I considered consulting the Lord about whether or not we should marry, even after my resolution to have a successful marriage. I thought God would be pleased with whatever path I chose, as long as I lived it for Him.

Three months later, we received the wedding video and photos in the mail. I opened the package. A cloud of disappointment loomed over me as I looked through the pictures. My dress was beautiful in each photo but my face and arms were hardly visible. Later that evening, Jack and I watched the video only to discover that it had been recorded with no sound.

Some might call it a sign. To me, the video and pictures served as confirmation of what I already knew in my heart-- I had sinned before the Lord when I married Jack. I wanted to make things right so I bowed my head in prayer and asked the Lord to forgive me. I told Him I was sorry that I hadn't heeded the three separate warnings He had sent my way (from my parents, my pastor, and the deacon), and asked Him if He would bless our marriage anyway.

Our First Year

Our first apartment was in the back of an old house in Canton, Michigan, the town where Jack had spent his high school years. I liked the ambiance and history of his hometown and was content to raise our future children there. In the first year of our marriage, Jack regaled me with tales of all the mischievous adventures he had initiated in school. We also joined a local church and became the Junior High Directors of a youth program.

I was so excited to share my first Christmas with Jack and his family that I put the festive decor up in the middle of November. I decorated the tree with two-inch ornaments that Stella had cross-stitched for us. When she came over to visit, she was unhappy that the ornaments weren't at eye level on the tree. A week later, Stella and Wayne asked to oversee all of our finances. I was appalled and did not consent to their wishes. As a result, they ceased all communication, refusing to speak to us.

I told Jack that we needed to show his parents that our love was unconditional. We would not be shaken by their attempts to control us or by their tantrums when we disagreed. Despite their wishes for no contact or gift exchange during the holiday season or at all until we honored their demands, we gave them their Christmas gifts anyway. A few days later, Wayne placed the unopened packages on our back porch.

Four months into our marriage, during the Christmas season, God blessed us with our first pregnancy. We were both thrilled to expand our family. I had wanted six children but after I gave birth, I had a hard time imagining going through the pain of labor and delivery again.

Jack's parents moved out of state two months before the baby was born. Our relationship with them remained strained because I would not give in and allow them to have control over various areas of our life. My heart was sad and felt empty at the realization that they were choosing not to celebrate the birth of their first grandchild with us.

I gave birth to my son three minutes before the clock struck midnight on September 9, 1990. 9-9-1990. The numerical significance struck me, as I reflected on the nine gifts and nine fruits of the Holy Spirit (**1 Corinthians 12:7-11; Galatians 5:22**). I hoped that my son would grow to experience and foster each of them. Peter was ten pounds and four ounces with bright, beautiful eyes. The nurse set him on my belly and I marveled at how my beautiful boy had the strength of an ox, as he held his head high and looked around the room.

Jack did not understand the cries of a newborn baby. He often lashed out at me if I let Peter cry for more than a few minutes. Ask any new mother, and she will testify to just how overwhelming life can be with a brand new little one. My husband's behavior, compounded on the exhausting new challenges of motherhood, caused me unneeded tension. I tried to avoid his angry demeanor by doing what I could to console my colicky baby.

On the Move

A few months after Peter was born, I opened a closet door and discovered that it was full of thick, green, fuzzy mold. We threw out all the wedding gifts that were stored in there and moved out as fast as we could.

Our new apartment was clean and spacious. Peter grew out of the colicky stage, which allowed me to enjoy his developing personality. When he would lie down for a nap, I would peer out the bedroom window, enjoying the peacefulness and the scenery outside of our home. On one such occasion, I gazed in wonder at a snowy owl perched on a branch of a towering pine tree. I couldn't take my eyes off of the beautifully majestic creature, and began to use those quiet moments of meditation to pray and thank the Lord for His blessings.

In the year 1991, as spring approached, Jack decided that he wanted to move to Florida to finish Bible college. One move with our new baby was fine, especially considering the circumstances with the mold, but two moves within six months of each other seemed unreasonable. I wanted stability for Peter so he could bond with family and friends.

I confronted Jack, and he hastily quoted a Bible verse that left me feeling guilty for desiring such a thing.

"**Matthew 10:37** says 'Those who love their father or mother more than they love Me are not worthy to be My followers,' so consider your desires and intentions," his sharp tone and icy glare reprimanded me as he molded the scripture to fit his purposes.

Our life together so far had been fun, joyful, and full of fond memories. I loved my new family, but I did miss the people from my hometown. Moving even further away would make my heart ache even more. I started to wonder if my resistance to moving was indeed fueled by my desire for those close connections. Was I, as Jack had accused, turning my back on the Lord's will again?

Meanwhile, I noticed that while Jack had been a good provider and friend, lately he had become more consistently confrontational, particularly after I expressed my thoughts about staying in Michigan.

As spring began to peek through the bleakness of winter with tiny green sprouts and blossoms, I walked into the office of our apartment complex and explained to the manager that we were going to move to Florida so that Jack could finish Bible college. I expected her to reprimand me for breaking our lease agreement. Instead, she reimbursed the full deposit and the rent payment for that month. I gasped in disbelief, "Ma'am, I didn't expect you to give us our money back."

With fear on her face, she stepped back.

"Oh, I don't want to get in the way of God's work, that's serious business," she said.

Speechless, I turned around to walk away. I was amazed that the Lord had just blessed our family with a large sum of money and wondered, *God, is it Your plan for us to move to Florida after all?*

THREE

RAGE

In the spring of 1991, we made our way to Florida. To help us get on our feet, we moved in with some old friends from college, John and Laura. Jack and John both worked to save money for college in the fall.

Each Sunday morning, Peter and I rode to church with Laura. The spring weather in Florida that year left a heavy frost on the land and destroyed a large percentage of the orange crops. The colder-than-normal temperatures made for many chilly mornings. To make matters worse, the car heater broke. We all huddled under warm blankets during our commutes. I wasn't happy about my baby being exposed to the frigid rides so I prayed, "Lord, is this really Your plan for our lives? What are we doing wrong?"

I continued to search for some sort of confirmation that I was helping to guide my family along the path we were supposed to be on.

On one particular Sunday morning, the bright sun woke me up. I tried to lift my head from the pillow but it pounded against my wishes.

Disappointed, I knew that going to church was out of the question. I spoke with a groggy voice, "Jack, I am too sick to go to church with you. Leave the baby here and go ahead without us."

Jack's demeanor quickly became aggressive. His red face appeared three inches in front of my eyes as he spewed out hateful words between his clenched teeth then declared, "I will take our son to church!"

I desperately began to negotiate with Jack because I wasn't comfortable with the baby being exposed to his anger. I had no strength to debate him, nor could I jump up to retrieve my baby. I laid my throbbing head down, stunned at my first glimpse of Jack's raw, angry emotion.

Jack scooped the baby up and got him ready for church in a matter of minutes. I lay there and wondered, *What did I do that was so horrible and where did this sudden burst of wrath come from?*

I heard the front door slam shut, and only then realized that Jack had left with Peter but hadn't bothered to grab the diaper bag or a bottle. I cried out to the Lord, "Please protect my baby."

Jack came home from church two hours later and filled me in on how things had gone without me.

"Peter cried on the way to church. I pulled over to the side of the road and picked him up to calm him down. When I put him back in his car seat, he began to cry again."

Sheepishly, with shame on his face, Jack continued to speak, confessing how he had let his anger get the best of him.

"I got mad," he said. "And when I buckled him into his car seat I noticed that my tie was caught in the buckle. I yanked it out too fast and he began to scream, but I think he's okay."

I swallowed my fear and looked Peter over. I could not make out anything different or unusual, until the next morning when I set him in the baby bath seat. That's when I noticed that Peter had two small red marks on his inner thighs.

Jack had fessed up but had obviously lost control of his emotions when he pulled the tie out from the seat buckle. I sought counsel from a woman in the church whose husband was also studying to be a minister, but was advised not to worry. I was told that it was probably a one-time thing. I vacillated between the advice and my motherly instincts. Was I overreacting? Or was I right to worry?

Sparks of Discernment

Second Opinion

If you feel uneasy with the counsel you have been given, you have the right to get a second opinion. If you are scared to share your situation with others, it's a good indication that you need a second opinion. Remember that it's for the safety of your child to ask for guidance.

"Remember that I commanded you to be strong and brave. Don't be afraid, because the Lord your God will be with you everywhere you go." (Joshua 1:9b).

On the Move...Again

That summer, our relationship with John and Laura came to an end, due to Jack's inability to compromise with them. We found ourselves facing homelessness until Steve and Sally, who we also knew from college, offered to take us in for a short time. Later, we found out that their house trailer was for sale. Jack decided to buy it.

Jack worked the night shift and I hardly saw him. The situation was awkward and our relationship was strained. I wanted to move back to Michigan to be near my parents and to give Peter the stability he needed.

All the joy and memories Jack and I had built together didn't seem to be strong enough to hold our marriage together. The stress was intense as a newly married couple with a baby. I knew that a place of our own would reduce our stress, so I prayed that we would be able to buy the trailer.

The Lord sent my uncle from Michigan to check out the condition of the home before we signed the papers for the final sale. He looked it over and warned us that it was not a suitable home for us. I was grateful that for the first time, Jack took his advice and was compliant to the wisdom that had been given to us.

Our friendship with Steve and Sally ended, since we were unable to purchase their home from them. I sensed that they felt used and unappreciated, and wished Jack and I had the means to make things right.

Moving in Florida

We made our fifth move into an apartment in Tampa, Florida. For the first time since the move from Michigan, Jack realized that we had no furniture other than our bed and Peter's crib, as we had previously been staying in already furnished homes. We found cardboard boxes and made end tables out of them, then covered them with old sewing material. We sat on plastic milk crates in the living room and had a few left to use as a dresser for our clothes. Jack happened to pick up two kitchen chairs and an octagon-shaped table that someone had for sale. He was excited about his find, even though the center glass piece was missing. I stood in silence and wondered how we could make it work, but Jack saw a challenge that he could rise to, and got to work.

I was delighted to see my husband back in action. There was an almost tangible shift in energy as his eyes lit up with possibilities and ideas forming for how to make the table usable. He ran out the door, to later return home with a large refrigerator box. He carefully cut out an octagon shape to fit the table. It was perfect. Cheerfully, I grabbed a tablecloth to cover the unsightly combination of wood and cardboard, then thanked him for the effort he put into it.

Everyone seemed happy and little Peter was free to run around in his own territory. Eventually he discovered where the pots and pans were. He would grab them with a sparkle of joy and a glint of mischief in his eyes. I was delighted to watch him create his own music. His happy spirit made my heart light up and helped me forget about the trials that Jack had put us through.

Jack worked a lot of hours, but the money he made was never enough. We made sure that the baby always ate, but Jack and I often went hungry. He came home one afternoon from work with double-stuffed chocolate cookies and soda pop. I was furious that he spent our last four dollars on junk food, especially since we had seven more days before his next paycheck.

I sat down at the kitchen table for dinner. I felt my elbows sink into the cardboard tabletop as I bowed my head to pray. Slowly, I sank my teeth into the cream-filled cookie, holding each bite in my mouth to savor the sweet flavor. After I finished my cookie, I gave in and grabbed a second one. Luckily for Jack, my hunger had dissipated and my anger ceased.

Jack was determined to keep me in the home to raise Peter, but our circumstances didn't allow for it. I found a job at a daycare center and was pleased that I could take my baby with me.

I didn't mind going to work but Peter did. He cried endlessly every day that we were there. I felt guilty when I left him in the nursery. He cried all day long for two weeks straight. I tried to take him into the toddler class with me, but he didn't like that either.

On the third week of being in our new apartment, I found myself angry with Jack because he bought a boom box with my first paycheck. We needed nutrition and a stable life, not a portable stereo. I felt that my efforts to work were unappreciated, so I quit my job. If Jack was going to use the money from my paycheck to purchase unnecessary items, I wasn't going to put Peter through any more crying sessions in the nursery.

On the fourth week in our apartment, I was awakened by a thunderstorm and thought I heard the sound of water running in the kitchen. I walked out to my clean kitchen and turned on the lights, then let out a scream of horror as hundreds of cockroaches ran for cover. The unsightly little creatures caused me to suffer a brief moment of mental shutdown.

I looked down and noticed a trail of water seeping from the kitchen closet. I opened the closet door and looked up. Bored through the roof was a two-inch galvanized pipe. I was furious that maintenance had overlooked the hole in the roof. I cleaned up the mess, while I thought about our financial situation and prayed. Why does it seem like life is so hard? I'd like to think we have sacrificed for the cause of Christ just as missionaries do. Only, Jack isn't in school and neither of us are doing anything for the Lord. "God, You gave us the money to move, why have our trials increased? What do You want us to do?"

I put the cleaner away then made my way to the bedroom. I stopped, then cringed as I felt cockroaches run beneath the carpet. "Why, Lord, does life have to be this way?"

The Lord heard my prayers. After three months of being hungry and poor, Jack surrendered and reached out to our mentors in Canton, Michigan for help.

Moving Back to Michigan

When our mentors, Melissa and Jason, arrived in Florida from Canton, we packed our clothes, kitchenware, and boom box into their van. I was glad to leave behind the furniture of crates and cardboard boxes, right alongside Jack's desire to attend college.

Our church family back in Michigan found us a little yellow house next to a cemetery. The quiet two-story home sat at the end of a dirt road next to an old barn. In years past, the groundskeeper of the cemetery worked from the little yellow house to maintain the memorial grounds.

I liked the home. The steep wooden stairwell had over thirty steps. I fell in love with the craftsmanship of the banister and enjoyed the challenge of dashing up and down the steps with my young legs, as I skipped two to three steps at a time. Just once I wanted to slide down the banister, but I was afraid that the fall might result in some serious damage, so I resisted the urge. I felt so free at that house. We had our own place, with a yard, and a swing out front under a beautiful maple tree that offered wonderful shade. Yet that home would prove to be the setting of some of the darkest times I'd have with Jack.

Things seemed to be falling nicely into place, but I soon realized that our parenting woes were not over. Though he wanted the baby to be quiet, Jack also wasn't fond of the way I jumped to little Peter's cries. It was the only way I could avoid Jack's irrational anger from rearing its ugly head. I found that it was best to keep my nine-month-old baby happy and quiet rather than experience another moment of rage from Jack. It felt like such a delicate balance and a dance on eggshells to keep him satisfied.

One summer night, we decided to turn in but Peter had other plans. He woke up and began to cry. I tried to get up to console him before Jack's anger reignited. Suddenly, I found myself trapped in a wrestling hold that became tighter and more painful as I tried to set myself free.

"You need to learn a lesson," Jack demanded. "Let the baby cry himself to sleep."

I tried to escape Jack's grip but he was too strong.

"Shelly, stop trying to get up or I will make it hurt more."

Sparks of Discernment

Crossing the Physical Line

To hold a person down against their will shows blatant disrespect and a lack of compassion. The passage below speaks of a peaceful life with a spouse who is loving and respectful.

"In the same way, husbands should love their wives as they love their own bodies. The man who loves his wife loves himself. No one ever hates his own body but feeds and takes care of it. And that is what Christ does for the church." (Ephesians 5:28-29).

TRIGGER
WARNING

TRIGGER WARNING to reader: this section contains animal cruelty. If you choose to avoid this section to protect your emotional and mental well-being, please skip ahead to the Sparks of Discernment on page 32.

My Cat

Jack ceased to show any joy in the time we lived in the yellow house, and his angry disposition increased throughout the summer. One afternoon he came home from work and began to look throughout the house for my cat, asking if I had seen the feline.

"No, Jack, he probably found a quiet spot to nap."

Jack continued to look for the cat before yelling, "Never mind, I found him!"

I heard the bathroom door shut and then the stomp of Jack's feet.

His sudden interest in the cat's whereabouts and the sounds that followed struck me as odd, but there was no way I could have imagined what was going on. Some time later, Jack made his way downstairs with the cat lifelessly cradled in his arms. His fur was mangled from the fight he put up.

"Jack, what did you do?" I cried.

He responded quickly in his defense, with no remorse in his heart. "He wouldn't cooperate and I'm sorry, I got carried away and strangled him with my bare hands."

I stared at my kitten in stunned silence. I didn't expect Jack to speak again, but he did. "You know what kinda disturbs me about the whole thing?"

My heart skipped a beat as I wondered if the news would get any worse. "No, Jack, what is it that disturbs you?"

"I feel as if I released an unusual amount of tension after I strangled the cat and I have never felt better!"

I could not believe what I had just heard. How could anybody heartlessly kill an animal in a fit of rage and feel good about it? What really bothered me about Jack's confession was the peaceful glow that overtook his demeanor as he gave a detailed account of how he killed the cat.

I couldn't respond to Jack's admission of unrepentant guilt and I was unable to accept what I had heard. Noticing the look on my face, Jack knew it would be a good idea to leave me alone and allow me to process what had happened.

I had grown up in a small farm town and was familiar with animals being put down due to sickness. However, I had never heard of anyone who had taken the life of an animal in a fit of rage. I was dumbfounded over Jack's actions, and because of what had happened, I became concerned for our safety.

Sparks of Discernment

Being Kind to All Creatures

God created animals for man to manage.

"Rule over the fish in the sea and over the birds in the sky and over every living thing that moves on the earth." (Genesis 1:28b).

"The godly care for their animals, but the wicked are always cruel." (Proverbs 12:10 New Living Translation).

Whenever cruel actions are done against any animal, one should report it and find a professional to talk to. Cruelty to animals is a warning that there are deeper issues that need to be resolved.

The Stairwell

The sound of crickets chirped outside and the smell of the chilly, fall air blew in through the windows. I wandered upstairs to tuck little Peter in for the night, then pulled the covers over my head and fell asleep.

A few hours later I was awakened by a high pitched wail. I sat up, cloudy-eyed and half asleep. I picked Peter up, then realized his forehead was hot with a fever. I took him out to the open stairwell landing, where his changing table was, to comfort him. When I took his temperature his cry turned into a scream, which woke Jack.

Jack charged toward me with a furious look. "What is going on out here?" he screamed.

I spoke with a nervous tone, "Peter has a fever."

"Well shut the kid up," he bellowed.

I felt threatened as Jack entered my personal space. He pushed my face until I was backed up to the edge of the stairwell landing. Briefly, I looked behind me to focus on the depth of the stairs, then calmly turned back to notice that Jack's red eyes had glossed over. I felt his slimy hot breath and spit on my face as it shot through his teeth while he shouted, "You better shut that kid up or I'll shove you down the steps."

Frozen due to space confinement and not fear, I was determined not to let Jack win this verbal duel. I challenged him, allowing the words to spew out with confidence, "Go ahead, I dare you!"

I look back now and realize that those weren't the wisest words to use, but I didn't want Jack to think that he could so easily make me fear him. Over the course of our relationship, I felt that I had developed valuable skills that allowed me to dodge his violent behavior, redirecting it to a more neutral state. But this time he triggered my anger button and I didn't back down. I was tired of all the mental maneuvering to appease him.

The next morning, Jack came downstairs for breakfast. I asked him about his reaction to Peter's cries in the night. He stared at me with disbelief written all over his face, then blurted out, "I blacked out and I don't remember a thing. Because we live next to a cemetery, I think I fell under the influence of the afterworld."

I didn't agree with Jack's theory. I felt the peace of the Lord over me while we lived in the yellow house. There was something deeper in Jack's life that was causing the emotional turmoil, and his anger was a result of that struggle.

As each day passed, Jack's insane episodes of rage increased. I confronted him about each of the angry events. He would always respond with the same answer.

"I blacked out and I don't remember a thing."

Jack's conduct left me to wonder, *Is he trying to excuse his actions and not take responsibility for his sin or does he have a detachment disorder?*

Sparks of Discernment

RAD

In my training to become a counselor, I came across a book on Reactive Attachment Disorder (RAD) called *When Love is Not Enough: A Guide to Parenting Children with RAD-Reactive Attachment Disorder* by Nancy L. Thomas.

Thomas explained that with severe cases of detachment, a person has difficulty forming authentic relationships and is unable to be genuinely affectionate with others. They learn to "act" as if they have attached.

Those who suffer from RAD can also be violent with animals and people. If you suspect RAD to be a problem with any member of your household, it is vital that you seek advice from your healthcare provider.

FOUR

THUNDERSTORMS OF LIFE

I rolled my eyes and groaned when Jack approached me with the news that we had been offered a cheaper rental on a large farm.

"Jack, we have moved five times in the last eleven months and I don't want to move again!" I cried out.

"But the landlord rents to those in financial need," he explained.

I knew we were poor, but I also knew our problems were deeper than simply being financial. They were emotionally troublesome.

Jack encouraged me to walk through the rental with him. I begrudgingly agreed, and as I stepped out of the car to see the place, I inhaled the smells of walnut and maple trees. Instantly, I was reminded of the town in which I grew up. My perspective began to shift as I was romanced by the wonderful nature before me. As we walked the property, I imagined our daily lives in the agricultural environment that offered a large yard with a swing set, a swimming pool, and a walking trail through the woods.

The charm of the farmhouse property won me over, and we moved yet again. As we still did not have many possessions, the move itself was a breeze. We began to settle into a new normal. Our new home was an apartment built just off of the main farmhouse, where our new landlords, the Berlays, lived. Being in such close proximity meant that any outbursts or bad behavior from Jack would likely be witnessed by the Berlays. Mrs. Berlay also had a habit of barging in to bring in the mail or simply to check on us. I felt safe, and I felt blessed. Jack did not quite share my view. In spite of the new apartment, Jack's theological views about God turned harsh. The shift seemed to be based on our Florida experience, but it also seemed as if his views vacillated from one extreme to another. Sometimes he saw God with grace and unconditional love, which, in his understanding, meant that he could sin and excuse his lustful behavior. He believed that his behavior was always forgivable because that's what God does-- forgive. And other times he saw God as vindictive and full of strict judgment. Jack could never find a peaceful balance between both views. It caused emotional turmoil that left an uncomfortable pit at the bottom of my stomach. But that wasn't the only thing growing in my stomach. As I struggled to keep our family strong, healthy, and afloat emotionally and spiritually, I found out that I was pregnant again.

Mr. and Mrs. Berlay were a godly couple that prayed for Jack's heart to soften. Jack seemed to take well to Mr. Berlay, and his influence caused my husband to be more sensitive and kind to me for a few months, in spite of his strict theological views. Mr. Berlay began to mentor Jack, and it gave me relief from Jack's angry disposition. However, that changed when Jack broke his foot at a volleyball game. It was at that point that our relationship took a turn into the valley of darkness.

Unable to meet the demands of his work with the volleyball injury, Jack lost his job. He was home with me, his pregnant wife, all day long in a small apartment. I waited patiently on him hand and foot, since his was broken. After Jack's pain subsided, he took off for the woods every day with crutches in tow, along with his hateful attitude. I was glad when he left for the day and I begged God to keep the rain away, to give me more time of peace in Jack's absence.

Six weeks later, Jack's foot was healed and he returned to work with a new job. Still, his mood differed from one situation to the next. He would appear to be remorseful about his behavior or actions, then with a flip of a switch, he would turn angry and judgmental. On good days, he was a carefree and fun-loving individual. I looked forward to the good days, but never knew when they would appear.

On Jack's first scheduled weekend off from work, we drove to town to shop for groceries. As we left the Berlay farm, I talked to him about his rude conduct and told him that it needed to stop. Jack slammed on the brakes and yelled, "I have every right to treat you however I see fit!"

Out of frustration, I yelled back, "I don't want to live with your rude behavior for the rest of my life. I am going to leave you!"

Jack snorted with arrogance, "Go ahead, but the baby stays with me!"

Jack had stopped the car and was waiting for me to get out, but there was no way I would leave Peter behind with such a loveless monster. I chose to sit in silence, accepting my reality. I was trapped in a relationship with a husband with whom I did not feel safe.

On the way to town, I talked myself out of leaving. I convinced myself that it would be better to stay with Jack to raise the children.

Tumultuous thoughts bombarded my mind as I attempted to find my way in what had become a very clouded situation.

How can I leave Jack with little Peter and another baby on the way?

We only have one car and I'm scared to drive by myself. If I leave Jack, I'm afraid he will stalk my family. Plus, I don't want him to have visitation rights to my babies without me around. I'm afraid he will hurt them.

Who would possibly hire me? I have been out of work for the last two years. What would I do?

I felt threatened by Jack and knew that if I left him, he would accuse me of being an unfit mother and do everything he could to make my life miserable. I feared he would take my babies and move so far away that it would be impossible for me to see them.

Because of my concerns, I willingly traded in my bold, outgoing personality for passiveness. My goal was to create a life of peace and safety in which the kids and I could survive. Over time, I saw the benefits of being dormant and staying neutral on all issues. Because of my behavior modification, I was able to endure life under Jack's dominance over a longer period of time than if I had continued to stand my ground.

Drug Runner

Jack switched jobs as many times as we moved. This time he found factory work. One evening after work, he mentioned that he had a friend named Jimmy. Jack told Jimmy that we needed a toy box.

He came home the next day and confessed that while he had hung out with Jimmy several times, this particular time he had swung by his place to pick up a toy box.

My smile disappeared as Jack laid the graffiti-painted box at my feet. He could tell by my reaction that I was not fond of the graffiti. The longer I remained silent, the more he disclosed. As he talked, he revealed that Jimmy was a drug runner, but that he'd simply gone over to his place to meet his buddies. Jimmy showed him around, then he grabbed the box and left.

I looked over the box, inspecting it thoroughly. It made me incredibly uncomfortable to think that my children would have something that came from a drug runner. I had a hard time imagining what Jack and Jimmy had in common that would lead Jack to be comfortable enough to spend time with him and accept the box from him, and my mind spun with chaotic thoughts.

"Are you running drugs?" I blurted out.

"No, I just went over to Jimmy's to pick up the box."

I was stunned at Jack's association with Jimmy. It just seemed so out of character for who I understood him to be. I thought about the verse, "Happy are those who don't listen to the wicked, who don't go where sinners go, who don't do what evil people do." **(Psalm 1:1)**. I had always felt that we were striving to surround ourselves with those who could help build us up and keep us on the right path, especially during the times of weakness, turmoil, and unrest within our family. On top of that, appearance was always very important to Jack, especially when it came to presenting himself as godly, moral, and unwilling to associate with those who chose to walk a path that our faith warned us against. We were always taught to love the sinner and hate the sin, but it seemed that Jack was quite comfortable and unbothered by Jimmy's sin.

I feared that Jack had walked down the wrong path with Jimmy and wondered if he would continue to be drawn to that same activity in the future.

Shortly after I ditched the graffiti box, I gave birth to our second son, Josiah, on March 16. 3-16-1992. Again, as with his brother, the numerical significance of my son's birth date caught my attention. **John 3:16-17** were some of my favorite verses, as they so simply and clearly stated God's unending love and grace for us.

"God loved the world so much that He gave His one and only Son so that whoever believes in Him may not be lost, but have eternal life. God did not send His Son into the world to judge the world guilty, but to save the world through Him."

Taking note of how the scripture reference numbers aligned with my new son's birthday, I felt that when God gave me Josiah, He was telling me that our family was being blessed with grace and love.

I loved my children and enjoyed entertaining them. Each day we would read books, have puppet shows, and sometimes bake cookies.

In spite of Jack's questionable secular friends, church became a place of hope and safety for me. I looked to them for comfort in my time of distress.

The church nursery had a painting on the wall entitled, *A Gift from God* by Ron Dicianni. The mother in the painting held her baby up to the heavens, while an angel of the Lord witnessed the occasion in the background. The lady in the picture inspired me to pray and dedicate each of my boys to the Lord while they slept in my arms. "Lord, these are Your children. Guide me in the way You want me to raise them. Prepare them to have a willing heart to serve You. I promise I will be sensitive to Your leading and direction in how You want me to guide them."

I didn't know God's plan for my children, but I knew I needed to prepare them to serve Him, just as Hannah did with her son Samuel, in **1 Samuel 1:21-28**.

Cold-Hearted Man

As I learned to demonstrate God's love toward Jack, he pushed me away and became heartless.

He forbade me from listening to radio preachers and accused them of being unbiblical and sappy. His judgmental attitude led to him eliminating words from his vocabulary such as grace, mercy, and unconditional love. He was quick to judge others and their relationships with God, but never stopped to reevaluate his own life.

Jack gloated when he spoke about the most recent development in his beliefs. "There's something special about me being chosen to go to heaven. I feel as if I am more important to God than you are or anybody else is. The crazy thing is, He doesn't expect me to read my Bible or witness to lost souls, since

He has the ability to show man what He wants them to know."

I felt the Holy Spirit grieve inside my stomach when Jack expressed his view of God.

"Jack, do you realize what you are saying?"

"Yes."

"Doesn't the eternal well-being of our children concern you?"

With a sharp tone Jack answered back, "No, I'm going to heaven and that's all that I care about."

Sparks of Discernment

God Loves

"God loved the world so much that He gave His one and only Son so that whoever believes in Him may not be lost, but have eternal life." (John 3:16).

"But God showed His great love for us in this way: Christ died for us while we were still sinners." (Romans 5:8).

"A thief comes to steal and kill and destroy,

but I came to give life-- life in all its fullness."
(John 10:10).

It is my belief that God sent His son, Jesus, to die on the cross for our sins so that we may have a fulfilling life. It is each person's choice to choose God or self. Remember that the gift of salvation is offered to each and every person. It's there for those who humble themselves and ask Christ to come into their lives to save them from their sinful actions.

College

For the second time in our marriage, Jack began to explore the option of going back to college to become a preacher. I was frustrated with his new doctrine and couldn't understand why he needed to attend school to share God's message of hope, when he believed that there was no need to witness to people.

Deep inside, I truly felt that Jack was playing a bad joke on me and didn't want to go back to college at all. I believed that all he really wanted to do was turn my world upside down and make my life miserable with yet another move.

Confirmation

A few days after Jack shared his desire to go back to school, he proved that he had no compassion or respect for me. I had just served him his favorite meal. He sat down at the kitchen table, sneered at his plate, then refused his food. I wrapped it up and put it in the fridge for later. After an hour passed, Jack complained of a headache and yelled at me, "You didn't feed me and now I have a headache!"

"You didn't tell me you were hungry. How am I supposed to know what you need if you don't talk to me?" I responded.

"I am your husband and you should know when I need food!"

I paused Josiah's nursing session to warm Jack's food up and bring it to him. He sat up in bed and voiced his disapproval, "Forget it! If you can't feed me before I get a headache then I don't want it."

He threw his plate across the floor and flung the freshly-folded laundry on top of the food mess. I sighed deeply as my stomach churned from the emotional turmoil that was in my spirit.

I had just given birth to Josiah ten days ago. I was exhausted and sore. Quietly I sobbed, allowing my hair to hide my face as I gently picked up the mess that Jack had made. While I had felt that his negative behavior in the past was a result of negative emotions, now, for the first time ever, I felt as if I had experienced deliberate disrespect from a husband who had promised to love and cherish me. Instead, he chose to break my spirit.

Sparks Of Discernment

SOPs

SOPs are the Standard Operating Procedures that are followed to create safety, security, and stability for firefighters. Whether one is fighting a fire, fighting to win a boxing match, or fighting to survive abuse, it is important to have your Standard Operating Procedures marked out so you are mentally prepared to initiate action for your own safety.

A boxer will think about his or her strategy, then practice for a win. The purpose is to win the boxing match in spite of the trials he or she will endure.

The trial of abuse can bring you down emotionally and cause you to lack hope for a better future. As a result, you or your children may have thoughts of self harm. It is vital that you stay connected with each family member and continue to keep the communication open with them. Watch for signs that indicate they are close to or have hit their breaking point, then get help immediately. Let it be your purpose to win the boxing match to end abuse, while you follow your family's Standard Operating Procedures to instill safety, security, and stability in your home.

Consider establishing your family's SOP around the following factors:

1. During your time of confusion and trials, keep your faith.

Many times during a family crisis, parents lose their faith in God. Kids notice the change and can become insecure and unsure of their future, making them more susceptible to addictions. Implementing change doesn't mean you have to pull away from the Lord. Instead, allow God to guide you. He is the only one who fully understands what you are going through.

2. Keep the family rules the same, unless they have been abusive, or expectations have been set too high.

Consistency can create a sense of security. Make a major, conscious effort to let the kids know that you appreciate them and thank them for helping you around the house. Give them grace if they goof up, and offer to help them complete a task. They are upset too, and need your understanding and compassion.

3. Eat as many meals together as possible (not necessarily with the abuser). Make it a positive experience instead of something the kids dread. Eating disorders are known to

develop during stressful times. Give your kids a fighting chance to overcome the effects of the abuse, instead of adding to it.

4. Go in and say good night to each child individually. They are more likely to talk when they are relaxed, so it's a great time to discuss how they feel about what has happened at school and in the home. Allow them to express their emotions without reprimanding them, and show empathy to let them know you care about them. You don't have to share anything with your abuser that will cause him to become angry toward the kids. Your children need to know that they will not be disciplined for how they feel.

FIVE

RADIATING ANGER

After Josiah turned three months old in the summer of 1992, we toured a college in Iowa. Jack liked what he saw, made his decision, and told me that I had one month to pack.

I felt distraught about making the move with an infant and a toddler, not to mention being 595 miles away from my hometown support group.

I was disappointed that we had to leave the quaint farm house in Michigan. But I knew that if Jack could actually finish school and grow to love me in the way that the Bible demonstrates, our future could be strengthened.

After three years and nine moves in our marriage, we arrived in Iowa. The fall semester began and Jack made many new friends. Most of these new friends were female, because after we'd arrived on campus, he'd changed his major from pastoral studies to education, and at that time, the field of teaching was dominated by women.

We lived on the college campus in the dorms designated for married couples. The family across the hall from our apartment had a lovely third-grade girl named Max. Max knocked on my door three weeks after we moved in and asked if my husband had a girlfriend.

"Why do you ask that?" I asked her.

"Because Jack was holding his girlfriend's hand at school today," she responded, referring to the school that she attended and at which the education majors did their student teaching.

I became sick as I thought about the possibility of Jack being unfaithful to me.

Jack invited me to chapel in the month to follow. He mentioned that he had a new friend he wanted me to meet. He spotted her on the sidewalk as she walked toward the chapel doors. Jack then turned around to yell at me as he ran toward her, "You stay here on the side of the road while I talk to her and don't come up there until I tell you to!"

Jack cheerfully ran to catch up with her. In the meantime, the hot sun began to beat against my angry body, as I held my two little babies. Jack and the girl chatted, she parted, and then I was finally invited to enter his presence. I was aggravated over Jack's rude and bizarre behavior, but chose to hide my feelings to avoid any public outburst of aggression. When we entered the church, he decided that his new friend would sit with us, and it was at this point that he finally introduced me to her, this friend who apparently was so much more entitled to his attention and kindness than I was.

Jack always seemed to think that I would not catch on to his new love interests if he introduced them to me before I became suspicious. But he always gave himself away when he acted as if I didn't exist and proceeded with a flirtatious attitude toward them.

One quiet afternoon while Jack was at work, Chelsea, a cheerleader from the college, called our house. I answered the phone.

Chelsea spoke, "Hi, uh, is Jack there?"

"No, how can I help you?" I answered.

"I want to speak to Jack," she insisted.

I rolled my eyes. I could only imagine what conversation she needed to have with Jack. "Chelsea, I am Jack's wife and I can relay the message to him for you. What is it that you need?"

Her voice was filled with angst as she once again declared that she needed to speak with him herself. I remained calm, cleared my throat, and once again denied her demand.

Chelsea sighed, and begrudgingly forced the words out of her mouth, speaking quickly. "I didn't get all the notes from class and I want to borrow Jack's."

"Chelsea, there are a lot of other students in the class who are not married," I spoke kindly but firmly. "Get your notes from them."

The next week Jack insisted that we go to a school basketball game. He had never cared for large social events, but this time he wanted to go and watch Chelsea do her cheers for the team. Disgusted, I held my tongue and rolled my eyes as I listened to Jack ogle over the formations and cheers that she had practiced for weeks.

Two weeks had passed when Chelsea the cheerleader knocked on our apartment door. I opened the door to six giddy cheerleaders on a mission to collect soda cans for a fundraiser. Chelsea wanted her girlfriends to meet Jack. She whispered to them, "Wait, he's here, you'll see him."

While I grabbed a few pop bottles for them, Jack swiftly entered the room like a hero and stood in the background as he shot a proud smile that made all the young girls sigh.

Burn Out

After three months of school, Jack experienced burnout. The combination of school, work, and his social interaction with all the girls proved to be too much and he quit his first semester. I was upset with Jack, in part because we still had to pay for the incomplete courses. I was also mad because I had given up my monthly visits to see my parents when we moved to Iowa, for what was looking more and more like another rash decision by Jack, made on a whim. I just couldn't understand why he had moved our family across the country to attend school, if he wasn't going to make the necessary sacrifices to achieve his goals.

TRIGGER
WARNING
TRIGGER WARNING to reader: this section contains physical intimidation and violence. If you choose to avoid this section to protect your emotional and mental well-being, please skip ahead to Reprieve on page 55.

Trust

We stayed in the college dorms, since Jack planned to enroll in the second semester with a changed major back to pastoral studies. He claimed to work overtime during his time off from school during the first semester, but our income never increased.

I grew to fear Jack when he came home from work. When would he lose it, and would I survive? His hate overshadowed my life. I felt threatened by his actions and couldn't trust him. I grabbed an object and hid it under the top mattress of my bed for self-defense. I didn't want to think about the need to defend myself but I knew how mean Jack could be. I so desperately wanted a healthy relationship with a loving husband, and there was a battle within me, where I knew the truth but wanted to believe anything else. As Jack's aggression progressed from nasty words and rude behavior to the occasional physical encounter, my fear grew. What I did not realize at the time was that my gut instincts were screaming at me, but my confused heart and mind wrestled them into submission. Similarly, Jack would use his body and domineering character to impose control and dominance over me. He had taken to jumping on me and holding me down in a choke hold until my air supply was cut off. In my mind, and likely in his as well, he was proving that I was no match for his strength.

Reprieve

I met Janine on campus during Jack's second semester of college. Her husband, Reggie, was a former military soldier who became a good friend to Jack, challenging him to pursue godly morals and principles.

I suddenly had a renewed hope for my marriage when Jack responded well to Reggie's guidance. Janine and I worked together to make family life functional, while our husbands poured their extra time into school and work. I felt that God had sent her my way to encourage me.

Jack and I spent many Sunday dinners with them, and the fellowship was sweet. Janine always arranged for her two older daughters to entertain Peter and Josiah while I took a few minutes to relax in a rocking chair near the kitchen. I watched Janine as she cooked potatoes, noodles, and roast beef. She always refused any offer to help, ordering me to sit down and put my feet back up. As I sat, I would watch the kids play outside through the window. I would often become distracted by the condensation that dripped down the glass panes. Each canvas seemed to have its own artistic flare. As I watched each droplet paint a unique path down the glass, I felt a hint of a memory stir within-- my creativity and expression, the music that used to swell within me until I could no longer contain my song. I wondered briefly where that magic had gone, then quickly answered my own question. *My musical and creative endeavors have been dormant because I only have the strength to focus on making it through each day, and providing the best life I can for my children. I'm in the mode of surviving, not thriving.*

Janine and her kids earned my trust, and we began to share childcare responsibilities with each other. I felt close to Janine.

She was a sane and soothing voice in the midst of my chaotic trials. She was the life preserver to my sinking ship when I felt emotionally locked up by Jack's oppression.

Small Town Diner

Jack's work life was ever-changing. He bounced around from job to job, and there was always a reason to leave one job to look for another. Sometimes he'd get bored, other times he felt he wasn't being given the respect he deserved, or he'd claim that others in his workplace just did not share his vision. Despite the lack of stability in income, Jack stood strong against any desire of mine to work outside the home. He vowed that he would make my life miserable if I tried to. One evening, he came home from work and mentioned that they were in need of a waitress at the small diner where he was working. I thought for sure Jack would allow me to work twelve hours a week, since we would be there together. When I made the suggestion, the look in his eyes revealed that he was stunned at the idea, as if it had never crossed his mind. After a moment, he gave a look of disgust and hesitantly stuttered, "Alright, we can try it."

I was excited to work two nights a week. Jack had always been in control of the finances, so when I received a paycheck, it would immediately go to him. When he gave me my first allowance, it was enough money to buy my first two pairs of jeans since we married.

Jack approached me after my third week at work and told me that I wasn't the right person for the job. He said that his boss offered him a pay increase if he could get me to quit. I never saw Jack's paychecks so I am not sure if he received a raise or if he just wanted me out of the way. Either way, my self-esteem plummeted and I felt that no one would ever hire me again.

That night I thought about how patient I had been while Jack tried to better himself with school. I wasn't sure why I'd put up with his mean temperament for so long and dreamed about what life would be like if the kids and I left him.

Fury

Spring was in the air and the kids were delighted to play outside. At nap time I washed all the curtains and finished the cleaning that I had started a few days before.

When the kids woke from their nap, we snuggled together on the couch to read books. After we finished our third story, the boys ran to play in their room. I watched as they pulled the toy blocks off the bedroom shelf. The freshness of the changing season, the joy emanating from my children playing, and the peace and productiveness of the day all culminated to create a happy and serene atmosphere. But it would not last long. And it would fade into a diminishing collection of happy moments all too often overshadowed by the ominous darkness my husband's presence brought to our lives.

Just as the blocks were coming off of the shelf, I felt the house rattle as the front door slammed shut. I went out to the living room to meet Jack. He growled as he glared at me, and without saying a word, he released his fierce and unprovoked aggression. He walked over to the wooden wall calendar that my mother had given me for my birthday, and smashed it to the floor.

Jack knew I missed my family and how much they meant to me, but he had clearly forgotten that I put more priority on relationships than I did on possessions. Jack looked up at me and waited to see if I would react. I stood still, emotionless and unwilling to give him any satisfaction. He never moved his eyes off me as he made his way to the kitchen, opened the cupboards, and threw pots and pans at me. I dodged every single one of them, but he caught me off guard with the next object he threw. Suddenly I was down, injured with a deep cut and a bruise from the corner of a stupid tissue box.

Jack stopped his tantrum and walked over to me with a look of what seemed to be concern. His personality had suddenly switched from angry tyrant to gentle, compassionate mate.

"Oh, did I hurt you?" he asked. "I didn't mean to do that. I am so sorry."

They were the first words that had come out of his mouth since he'd walked in the door that day. I paused, then straightened my body, gathering my dignity.

My dignity and resilience were nothing that Jack was interested in putting up with. The tyrant and tantrum immediately returned, and he threw the rocking chair in Peter's direction. Instinctively, I stepped into the path of the airborne chair to protect our two-year-old son. The chair's round, wooden base fell on my leg.

Jack stopped again and spoke calmly, "Sorry, I didn't mean to hit anyone, are you okay?"

I nodded my head with a yes, keeping my composure and unwilling to stoop to his level of unhinged emotion and reactive hysteria. *When is he going to end his temper tantrum?* I wondered.

Next he hoisted the highchair up and threw it five feet into the living room. The wall proudly held the legs of the highchair with a tight grip and resisted to let go until Jack firmly yanked it from the wall.

I showed no fear in response to Jack's anger. In my mind, I was done dealing with his uncensored, childish behavior. He noticed that I was not intimidated by his dramatic presentation so he tried a new approach. He walked up to me and hissed through his teeth with a deep growl in his voice, "If you ever leave me, I will hunt you down and I will kill you!"

I knew I needed to get away from this angry monster but I wasn't sure how I could make that happen. I began to pray, "How do I get out of this situation?"

The Lord pressed upon my heart to save two hundred dollars to pay for bus tickets for myself and for the children. I scrimped and saved what I could from our tiny grocery budget and continued to pray about where we could start a new life without having to worry about Jack's death threat. I knew that once we were safe, I would need to change our names and find work. I had the faith and peace needed to make that plan a success, but I wondered if we would be able to get away from Jack before things worsened.

A couple days later, there was a knock on my apartment door. It was Janine. She stood bewildered when she noticed the holes in our living room wall. Her eyes widened as she asked what had happened.

I quickly and quietly answered her, "Um, Jack threw the highchair into the wall."

Jack overheard the conversation and forced a laugh, jumping to tell his version of the story. He spoke as if he were in disbelief over his own actions.

Janine hesitated after hearing what we each had to say. "Is everyone okay?"

My eyes shifted from her gaze as I hung my head. "Yeah,

we're okay," was all I could muster.

Sparks of Discernment

Internalized Stress of Abuse

"I stood still, emotionless and unwilling to give him any satisfaction."

Throughout the 17 years I was married to Jack, I chose to show no fear. Instead, I internalized my feelings so he wouldn't think I was weak. Over the years, he ridiculed me and demanded that I stop whenever I felt the need to cry, be angry, or be irritated.

I was not allowed to express any emotions that he deemed to be negative. I still felt them and wanted to express them, but I didn't because of the repercussions that would befall me if I disobeyed Jack.

Not being given any space to express my emotions caused a consistent amount of cortisol to be dispensed into my system, from the stress that I was under. The physiology of how my body works changed because of this. My immune system became compromised and I struggled with digestive issues, allergies, illnesses, and low blood sugar. My boys also suffered from compromised immune systems which resulted in food allergies, asthma, and eczema.

When you're under abusive influences, you focus on how to get through it. The sole focus is survival, or just getting by. Instead of enduring it like I did, consider the consequences that it could have on you and your children later in life.

If you need help, start with your family doctor. They are required by law to keep all information confidential. Also, if you talk to your doctor when you're emotionally strung out, he or she can make a note of it. Upon request, the documents can be used to your advantage in the court of law, if your situation becomes unmanageable or dangerous.

Father's Day

In June of 1993, we heard that our former dorm parents from the Florida Bible college had come to town. Sean and Jen's roles as dorm parents in Florida were much like that of resident assistants, with Sean tending to the needs of the young men and

Jen in charge of the young women. It created something of a family dynamic, and we looked up to them as role models. Now they had moved to town so that Sean could take a few more college classes. In the meantime, he was hired to pastor a nearby church. Jack decided to switch churches to leave behind our good friends Reggie and Janine, to join Sean and Jen. Our new routine consisted of Sunday afternoons in fellowship with them at their house. Jack's new goal was to go back and finish college, and fulfill his pastoral internship under Pastor Sean.

On Father's Day, one month after Jack's last temper tantrum, I found myself rushing around to make sure everything went well on his special day. I was determined to handle the morning's duties so that he could have the chance to kick back a bit. In order to get everything done that I needed to do before we left for church, I knew that something would have to wait until later. I informed Jack that he would get his Father's Day gift when church was over. He seemed unconcerned by this as he leisurely went about his morning. While he relaxed, I got the kids ready for church, then ran to the kitchen to put a hash brown casserole together. As soon as the frozen hash browns and other ingredients went into the glass dish, the glass dish went into the preheated oven, and I hastily moved on to the next task at hand. But as I filled the diaper bags, I was startled by a loud bang that sounded like a gun.

"What was that?" I called out to Jack.

"I think it was the oven," he responded.

A dark cloud loomed over me as I walked over to the oven and slowly opened the door. I stared at the catastrophe on the oven floor. The glass dish had exploded into a thousand tiny pieces and the casserole lay in a heap on top of the broken glass. My joy was extinguished as I attempted to discuss the clean-up options with Jack. My first idea was to throw the oven out completely and replace it with a new one, but instead I found myself scraping the casserole remains from the oven floor with a spatula as Jack looked on, laughing.

Exhausted from the events of the morning, I grabbed some hot dogs to take for lunch and threw them into the diaper bag. For all of my effort to give Jack a pleasant, relaxing, carefree Father's Day, the day was off to a rocky start and I was feeling a bit defeated.

After the Sunday service was over, we walked over to the pastor's house to prepare for dinner. Upon our arrival, Jack abruptly stormed past me. Recognizing an oncoming moment of rage, I waited for the diaper bag to come flying across the yard. I had grown accustomed to anticipating miscellaneous objects being thrown around or at me.

The kids and I went down to the guest room of the pastor's cool basement to rest for a few minutes until Jack came down to join us. He pitched a fit, whipping his tie off in a wild fashion.

"Jack, what's the matter?" I uttered, not entirely keen on hearing the answer.

"I can't believe you forgot to recognize me on Father's Day!"

I stood in disbelief as I slowly pulled the gifts out of the diaper bag. I handed him his Father's Day card, only to have him whip it back at me. I winced with pain as the corner of it cut my arm.

"Forget it, Shelly. If I have to remind you, then I don't want anything from you."

While I waited for Jack to calm down, I remembered a verse, "A soft answer turneth away wrath but grievous words stir up wrath." **(Proverbs 15:1 KJV)**.

Gently, I reminded him that I had planned to give him his gift after the church service was over.

"Stop right there, I don't want to hear it!" he shouted, and he ran up the stairs, skipping two steps at a time.

My little boys stared at me with fear on their faces. I knew I needed to reassure them that everything was going to be okay. I held back my tears for as long as I could to give the boys security, but then began to sob uncontrollably.

SIX

UNSTABLE FOUNDATION

After three and a half years of marriage, Jack proved that he had something of a conscience when he confessed to six affairs.

"Shelly, I'm sorry I cheated on you. Will you forgive me?"

"Where do you want to go from here, Jack?"

"Well, I want to get help but I don't want to get kicked out of college," he answered, clearly most concerned about his status and reputation at the Bible school.

He had just dropped an emotional bomb into an already unstable environment, and I needed to get away from him for a few minutes. I retreated to the bathroom and attempted to make sense of what my world had become, but I just felt numb inside, unable to process my emotions. I wanted the relief that would come with the release of tears, but they refused to fall.

I rubbed my belly for comfort. Nobody knew. She would be born into this reckless situation and I knew that she could sense my grief. I was tough and felt I could handle Jack's mistreatment but I wondered how his anger would affect my children. Or had it already? *One thing is for sure,* I thought. *After I give birth I'll have my tubes clipped. I don't think I can handle more than three kids without Jack's help.*

I came out of the bathroom and walked into the kitchen. Jack walked up beside me. He opened his arms with acceptance but was emotionally distant. It was as if he were going through the physical motions of repentance but the morality and sincerity of it all stopped at the surface.

I felt nothing. I wasn't happy or sad. All I knew at that moment was that I should clean something, because that would help to clear my head.

Jack stood on the outskirts of the kitchen as I hustled about. "Shelly, how am I going to get help?" Obviously, he was more worried about how his past actions affected his future than how they affected me. His question annoyed me.

"I don't know Jack, I'll talk to the pastor's wife and get her advice."

The following Sunday, Jack shared his dilemma with Troy, a deacon at church. Troy's father, Donald, was a pastor in a town far enough away that Jack was comfortable getting counsel from him, without the fear of his infidelities getting out into the network of people he knew.

The next day, Pastor Donald sat in our living room on a kitchen chair, while Jack sat on the floor in a corner with his face covered. Perhaps truly ashamed, or perhaps just playing the part, he recounted his adulterous tales. I ran my fingers through my long brown hair, uncomfortable with the details of the affairs. I couldn't tell if I was ill from the pregnancy or from the information he shared.

Every new detail opened a new wound for me as Jack continued to share his life of sin. I felt as if he had punched me in the stomach when I discovered that a portion of our income had been used to pamper his dates.

I recalled the mental boxing match I had felt I needed to fight to marry Jack back when I had faced opposition to our marriage. I never dreamed there would be a boxing match in my own living room, with my husband. We were supposed to be on the same team. We were supposed to support, encourage, and cheer each other on. Instead, he had become my opponent and was pummeling me with emotional blows as I clung to the side ropes of the boxing ring.

I tuned him out to escape the details of his affairs and prayed, "Lord, now I see why You didn't want this marriage to happen. And now I'm scared Jack will hunt me down and kill me, if I take the children and run."

I reflected on the advice that Miss Prudence, my college professor, had given me. I asked myself, *Why should I give Jack a hot meal, respect, and intimacy when he can't give me a reason to trust him?*

Jack still thought that he was being called to be a pastor. But I didn't think he would be a positive role model for any community.

I snapped out of my trance when Pastor Donald's voice boomed. "Shelly, nobody needs to know about these affairs Jack has been involved in." He paused then looked down at the floor before he spoke again, only this time with softness, "Jack confessed his sin, God forgave it, and so should you."

He then gave me a stern look of discipline and disgust as he shifted the weight of his body in his chair and cleared his throat.

"Shelly, you need to make yourself more attractive. Look at your clothes. My wife would never be caught wearing a sweater with jeans. You should wear a dress every day with jewelry, stockings, and dress shoes. Go look at your hair. You need to do something with that and you need to wear more makeup."

In the corner of my imaginary boxing ring, I stood up to gather my strength from Pastor Donald's last few words that took a deep jab at my heart. He looked over the top of his glasses and spoke louder with his last sentence, "No wonder Jack has struggled with infidelity, look at you, this is your fault!"

I tried to focus on our visitor but I was in a state of shock. I couldn't believe that the pastor showed compassion toward Jack but reprimanded me.

I waited for my turn to speak, to defend myself, but I wasn't given the opportunity. Instead, I returned to my thoughts, the one place I was able to retaliate to the absurdity before me.

What? If the fault is somehow on me, but Jack makes the money, then when is he going to take responsibility for me and buy me the makeup, wardrobe, and gym membership he is talking about?

I think there are some deeper psychological issues here that exclude my appearance. We are talking about a man who has had six affairs. Obviously he needs intervention, not excuses to enable him.

Mentally, I pinched myself as I continued the silent conversation within the walls of my mind. Is this really happening? Why is this man defending Jack's sinful behavior and blaming me?

I no longer trusted Jack and I didn't care if he left me. The only thing I worried about was the well-being of my children. I had been ready to make a change, but fear and fatigue took over, and I decided to buy diapers with the money I had saved for the bus tickets. A sense of relief washed over me, now that the money was gone and I no longer feared that Jack would find it and end my life.

Sparks of Discernment

Leadership and Support

Because the pastor accused me of being at fault for Jack's unfaithfulness, I can understand why so many people never go back to church again.

Jeremiah 23 assures us that God will deal with wrongful leadership and we must trust Him to complete that work. However, we have authority to set boundaries for those who do not show us a spirit of respect and understanding.

We also need to pray for pastors to have a spirit of discernment concerning victims of abuse. Sometimes leadership is unaware of how their viewpoint comes across and it may cause a victim to avoid church altogether. Pastors may not understand what a victim has been through, and may offer advice that causes victims to feel unsafe.

A friend once shared that a campfire represents a church. The embers of the campfire are the congregation. When we come together in church, the embers glow brighter and hotter for the Lord. But the longer an ember stays out of the campfire, it dims, as the member that it represents becomes discouraged, his or her hope diminishing.

This analogy really hit home for me, and as I meditated on it, I was able to apply it even further. When a log gets added to a campfire, there are always a few embers that blow away in the wind. That log represents a trial being dropped into the church, such as a family with the issue of abuse. Sometimes the victims of abuse are the embers that get pushed out of the church because they are misunderstood. Unfortunately, these embers are the ones that get rejected and it causes their light for the Lord to go out, in the midst of a very confusing and dark ordeal. Be mindful of these lone embers.

There are two types of fires-- those that must be extinguished and those that must be stoked. Abuse is a damaging fire that must be fought against at all costs. But the fires of fellowship, the right to a free, fulfilling, peaceful life, and the will to survive are those fires that must be fed, tended to, and regularly fueled.

Watch for those who need the healthy fire most. Instead of ignoring the issue or deeming it too uncomfortable to discuss, be willing to offer guidance, a listening ear, and prayer. Help that ember find the resources she or he needs to once again grow into flame.

Flood of 1993

The summer was humid in the seventh month of my third pregnancy and it left me with frizzy hair and an overheated body. I searched for comfort but nothing would suffice.

That summer of 1993, the ground was still drenched from rain and the current spring ice melt. The combination of soaked earth and broken levees in the states of Illinois, Iowa, Kansas, Minnesota, Missouri, Nebraska, North Dakota, South Dakota, and Wisconsin created disaster. From July 11 through July 22, the Raccoon River took over the Des Moines, Iowa water treatment plant and city officials were forced to shut it down. This left us without water or power.

Many volunteers worked together to fill sandbags downtown

and help where assistance was needed. We had friends report seeing coffins rise above ground level and float down the river path from the cemetery. Thankfully, volunteers respectfully helped to rectify that situation.

I always wanted to experience what it would be like to live in the 1800s, but I changed my mind when I found myself without a hot shower, no way to brush my teeth, and unable to cook with tap water. I even had to do the unthinkable and not flush the toilet, which turned my pregnant stomach sour.

Just before Josiah had been born, Stella had changed her tune and decided to allow us back into her good graces. Since Jack was out of work due to the citywide shutdown, his parents invited us to visit them in Colorado. I was grateful for their offer and looked forward to drier territory.

On the drive to Colorado, Jack became overwhelmed with grief from a phone conversation he had with his father about Jack's unfaithfulness. Wayne thought Jack's behavior was a result of the way he was punished as a young boy.

I didn't agree with the style of discipline Wayne and Stella had chosen for their kids nor did I adhere to it. They would swiftly administer punishment without warning, explanation, or guidance regarding the offending party's misstep. I was raised with a spirit of patience, love, and understanding and I chose to raise my children in the same manner.

Jack, however, was emotionally traumatized from physical abuse. The aggression and hate Jack had toward me now made sense. Despite having spent the bus money, the constant battle within me raged, and I often imagined a happy life with my children, away from Jack. But now a new factor entered the equation. I asked myself, What am I supposed to do now that

I know Jack was abused as a child? Should I leave him after the baby is born or should I help him work through his emotional trauma?

We spent two weeks with Jack's parents, and despite the rocky start, it was overall a nice trip. Our young boys got to spend time with their grandparents, and Jack acted as if the difficult phone conversation that he'd had with his father had never happened. At the end of the two weeks, when the power had been restored throughout the city, we went home to await the arrival of our newest family member.

Samantha

Two months later, on the sixteenth day of September, I gave birth to a baby girl named Samantha. 9-16-93. I couldn't keep the smile from my lips when I connected her birthdate to those of her brothers'. Peter's significant number was 9, and Josiah's significant numbers were 3 and 16. Samantha's birthday included numbers from both her brothers' birthdays. It was as if her birthday tied them all up nicely in a beautiful bow representing all my babies. I knew that she would be blessed in grace and love, as well as with all nine spiritual gifts.

I had an uneasy sense about Samantha's health and watched her carefully. She seemed sluggish and didn't eat very often. Her cries were weak and it was hard to wake her to nurse.

Three days after I brought her home from the hospital, the phone rang. The nurse on the other end was doing a follow-up call to check on Samantha. She asked me a series of questions, all of which I could not give a positive answer to.

My stomach turned when I heard the last question, "What

color is her skin?"

I answered, "She looks more yellow than when we first left the hospital."

The nurse instructed me to press my finger on her tummy and quickly remove it. I then gave her the results of the underlying pigment that appeared. "Her skin is pumpkin orange."

The nurse spoke with a firm but nervous tone, "Bring her into the hospital immediately."

Jack was at work when I got the call from the nurse. I called him and told him how urgent it was for Samantha to get to the hospital.

"I don't know what to tell you," Jack replied without concern. "I can't take time off from work. You're going to have to call for a cab."

I stood deep in thought as I tried to grasp the reality of my situation. I was on my own. I had no money to pay for a cab and I lacked three car seats for three children, and one was very ill. I was perplexed and overwhelmed with urgency for Samantha's life.

In desperation, I prayed. "Lord, where is Jack? Why has he abandoned us? Please help me!"

It was then that my friend, Mariah, came to mind. I called her and she promptly rescued us.

My innards began to roll with anxiousness as we found ourselves at war with time, when a giant wasp flew into the car. Mariah gasped and pulled the car over to the side of the road. We quickly pulled the kids out of the car and shooed the wasp out with a paper that Mariah grabbed from the glove compartment. We were both relieved that the situation was under control without injury to baby Samantha or her brothers, but the obstacle that had added time to our journey had also added more anxiety to my already worried mind.

We entered the hospital and walked to the front desk. The nurse looked at me and spoke with emphasis, "What took you so long to get here?"

"I didn't have a car," I quickly responded, anxious for Samantha's care to get underway. To me, the obstacles of transportation to the hospital had already been surpassed, and it was time to take care of my baby. The nurse's question felt like a waste of precious time.

"I would have sent a paramedic to pick you up if I had known that was the problem," she said with disappointment.

The nurse took Samantha to a room and ordered lab work to be done immediately. Mariah had gone back to the apartment with the boys, and I sat alone with the doctors as they informed me that a normal bilirubin count was in the single digits, with some at 10 or slightly higher. Cause for concern started around 15 or 16. The room grew silent before they continued the prognosis. Samantha's bilirubin count was 32.

The group of doctors tried to remain calm as they informed me that Samantha could lose her ability to see and hear because of her high bilirubin count. With urgency, they shared two options of treatment. The first option was the bilirubin lights, but they were concerned that they wouldn't work fast enough, before impairment set in. The second option was a blood transfusion.

I didn't have peace about a blood transfusion. I was assured it was a safe and effective solution, but my personal fear of bloodborne pathogens overtook my mind. I couldn't stop thinking about the risks of my baby contracting something serious, like HIV. At the time, I assumed that HIV was my biggest fear for her because it was such a well-known virus. My anxious spirit wouldn't let it go even though I knew a blood transfusion would be an immediate fix to her condition. However, if she was diagnosed with HIV, she would have to deal with that for the rest of her life. I pleaded with the Lord and asked Him to bless the use of the bilirubin lights.

Mariah made frequent visits to the hospital to see baby Samantha and me. She always brought me food and a change of clothes. She even let me borrow her Bible.

Stella and Wayne came to town to take care of the boys while I stayed with Samantha. I talked to Jack briefly a few times on the phone. It seemed as if he worked in another country. When I prayed, I knew why he didn't bother to check on baby Samantha. He was preoccupied with matters of his life that he kept separate from us. Perhaps it was another woman. Perhaps he had stopped caring about our family. I wasn't concerned in the least bit. I had enough love in my heart to care for my three babies without his help.

I stayed with my baby to feed her and change her diapers. In my spare time, I caressed her skin and prayed over her, so she would know that she was loved and cared for.

God heard my prayers. Samantha was healed with the use of the bilirubin lights and never lost her hearing or eyesight from the high bilirubin count.

One month after Samantha was treated, a local newscast informed the public that there were contaminated bags of blood stored at the blood bank. They warned the public of the possibility of being infected with HIV if they had had a blood transfusion in the past few months. I was thankful God heard my prayers and that I had listened to His leading.

In December of 1993, Samantha turned three months old. Jack took a semester off and moved our family off campus, 26 miles away from the school. I had no friends and no car.

I didn't understand why we had to move away from my only support system, especially since we were given prior permission to live on campus, in spite of Jack's leave of absence. I tried to discuss other options with him, but his decision was firm and he would not allow me to voice my opinion.

The kids and I were tucked away in our tiny apartment. Jack forgot about us and hung out with the guys from work after he completed his shift. We rarely saw him. Because of his absence, life was peaceful, stable, and good, even without my support system.

Sparks of Discernment

No Menstrual Cycle

During my third pregnancy, I had decided that it would be my last one. I previously made plans with my doctor for surgery to prevent any future pregnancies, until I was prompted by the Holy Ghost not to. I went through with the procedure anyway, for I was sure that three were all I could handle by myself.

After I had Samantha, the stress from being married to Jack was so intense that I never had another period until a month after I left him, which was 13 years later. The Holy Ghost was right, I didn't need to worry about it because He shut my womb.

It is important to recognize just how powerful abuse can be, even if your abuser never lays a hand on you. You may not realize how much the stress from abuse changes the physiology of the body. However, if your menstrual cycle isn't regular, you should always have it checked by a doctor in case of other complications. And if your body is indeed physically reacting to your stressful lifestyle, discussing this with your doctor could be the first step toward getting help and breaking free from the chains of abuse.

SEVEN

HAZARDOUS SITUATION

*I*n the fall of 1994, Jack renewed his commitment to finish college and we moved back to housing on campus. A few months later, he lost his zeal to complete his degree.

Jack called his parents to get advice for his dilemma. They had moved to Texas since we had last seen them, and Stella took the opportunity to persuade Jack to move to Amarillo, near them. Jack's mother ended the phone conversation with one last statement that stuck with Jack.

"You need to stop putting so much effort into earning a degree and focus on the needs of your family."

I was filled with anxiety about a move across the country with three babies, especially not knowing, once again, what life had in store for our family in yet another new and unfamiliar environment where Jack had control.

The beginning of the trip went well enough, until our moving truck blew a tire on the expressway in Kansas.

I cautiously walked across the four-lane expressway with our three children in tow. My anxiety soared as I attempted to quickly usher my babies to safety. We made it to a mechanic's shop on the other side of the expressway and sat in the lobby while Jack stayed with the truck. A few hours later the tire was fixed and we were ready to roll down the expressway to our new home.

We hit torrential rains for the remainder of our trip and were blessed to arrive safely at Stella and Wayne's. When Jack opened the back door of the moving truck, I cried. Before we had left for our trip, Jack had tied a clothesline across the back of the truck to hang our wardrobe. The rope broke during our travels and all the clothes sat on the floor of the truck, covered in mud.

We stayed with Stella and Wayne for a few weeks, long enough to wash all the muddy clothes and catch up on each other's lives. During that period, we looked for a rental and found a mobile home to rent in a nearby town.

Once I felt settled, my mood improved and I began to feel emotionally strong. I was in control of my domain, and that brought joy and positivity.

The kids and I spent a lot of time outside in the warm sunshine under the open blue skies of Texas. We rode our bikes on the paved roads of the trailer park and played in our new yard. Jack was around more and the kids began to connect with him.

Jack became an assistant manager at a nearby restaurant in the fall of 1995. His new position seemed to boost his self-esteem and he seemed to be happy in our marriage.

Stella, ever so pleased that we had moved into her vicinity, rewarded us for what she perceived to be following her orders. My mother-in-law doted on us and bought everyone new clothes. I was glad to toss the outdated apparel and felt like a new person with a renewed sense of confidence.

Stella introduced me to the ladies of her church. I felt at home there and made many friends. The church had a strong bond within its congregation and a bold sense of accountability, something that both Jack and I desperately needed.

Meanwhile, Jack was meeting with his parents frequently to work through his traumatic past. Something in him seemed to change as he left behind his tyrannical behavior and unfaithful ways.

I gained confidence in my relationship with Jack and decided to hire a babysitter. I wanted to surprise him with a visit while he was at work. I walked into the restaurant and slowly let go of the front door. I watched, stunned, as Jack screamed and threw pots and pans at his employees. I couldn't believe it, he'd flipped his lid.

When Jack spotted me, he stopped yelling and resumed a demeanor of peace. The whole scene had happened so quickly, I thought my mind had played a trick on me.

Obviously, work had become Jack's new outlet for the anger and frustration he felt inside his stormy soul.

Salvation

Our new church was located a few miles outside of Amarillo, just off of the main highway. The pastor trained men for the ministry, and Jack felt that he would benefit from the program. In the fall of 1995, Jack joined the ministry team. We moved into a house across the street from the church, so he could better serve the community.

Jack quickly became discouraged with the menial tasks he was asked to do and became doubtful about his decision to train for God's work. In spite of Jack's inconsistency, the Lord worked in both of our hearts for spiritual growth.

Jack and I both understood that we were sinners and had asked Jesus to cleanse us from our sins during our childhood years, and were baptized. My salvation took place at age eight. Jack's salvation took place at ages five, thirteen, and again at age seventeen, perhaps so redundantly because of guilt for recent transgressions, out of fear or uncertainty that he wasn't truly saved, or a combination of those reasons.

In my mind, Jack proved that he was saved because every once in a while, he would demonstrate what I understood to be godly traits.

What happened next shocked me and shook my inner core. Jack had shown that he was capable of ugliness in the past. I believed it was up to me to show him love and forgiveness. And what would be revealed to me was beyond what I would ever imagine was possible from a person who had claimed to have surrendered to the Lord.

It was November of 1995, and with my birthday just a few days away, I was excited to share it with my church family. The pastor finished his Sunday speech that morning and ended with a message of salvation. He read, " 'Also, I will teach you to respect Me completely, and I will put a new way of thinking inside you. I will take out the stubborn hearts of stone from your bodies, and I will give you obedient hearts of flesh. I will put My Spirit inside you and help you live by My rules and carefully obey My laws.' So says **Ezekiel 36:26-27**."

Jack's fingers tightly gripped the pew as he listened to the scripture reading. I watched him from the corner of my eye and noticed that his face was white, like that of a ghost. I became concerned and thought he might faint, so I leaned in and asked him if he was okay.

Without an answer, Jack dashed off and left the church before we finished the final song. I picked the kids up from the nursery, then walked over to the house to find out what had gotten into Jack to cause his sudden departure.

There he sat, on the top step of the back porch, with his Bible open on his lap. I stood next to him, but he acted as if I didn't exist.

Though this behavior was out of the blue for how things had been going in the most recent months, it was reminiscent of another period of our marriage. Something about his behavior nagged at my instincts, and I began to ask him questions about the possibility of an affair with a young lady at work. He snapped out of his trance, jumped the fence, and ran back to the church.

My anxious spirit welled up inside me as I fed the kids lunch and laid them down for a nap. Two hours later, Jack walked up to the front door with the pastor.

Pastor Alex sat calmly in our living room and gave me a brief overview of what they had talked about in his office. He informed me that Jack had just prayed for salvation. The pastor paused for a moment then cleared his throat.

"Jack has more news he needs to share with you. My wife and I are here to make sure nothing gets out of control."

My stomach tightened and churned as I listened to Jack admit to another affair. Before I could process the information, he asked for my forgiveness.

I sat numb, remembering that he had asked for my forgiveness just two years ago, for the affairs he'd had in Iowa.

As Jack's story began to unfold about his involvement with the most recent young lady, I realized I was back in the dreaded emotional boxing ring I thought I'd left behind in Iowa.

"When Pastor read **Ezekiel 36:26-27**, I realized that I had a hard heart and had never before been convicted about my sin," Jack was saying. "The verses say that if I'm saved, the Lord will give me a tender heart and He will help me to walk in His statutes."

In spite of how the verses spoke to Jack, the news of the affair affected me like an emotional beating that started with a series of combination punches. The first hit was a left jab-- Pastor Alex's disposition when he told me that Jack had something more to confess. Then came the straight right as Jack admitted to the affair, followed by the left hook as he expected my forgiveness right away, before I had processed the fresh pain. Once again, I felt cornered and was unable to punch back as I sat in shock, just as I did with Pastor Donald in Iowa.

I sat quietly as I took each emotional blow. When Jack finished his confession, I was expected to instantly forgive and go on with life as if nothing had ever happened.

I managed to utter two syllables before Pastor Alex cut me off with a sharp statement. I realized that once again I would not be given a chance to voice my comments or concerns. It was all too familiar, and just like before, it was then time for me to absorb my thoughts and feelings, as my mind was the only place where they were permitted.

Is this time any different from our first boxing match? Is Jack actually going to change? Is this going to be the end of all his mind games and instability? Did Jack make a decision to follow Jesus just because I exposed the possibility of an affair?

I remained silent, stunned, and sick to my stomach. I tried to ask Pastor Alex a question but was silenced for a second time. I felt as if I were being treated like a child who was too immature to know how to properly express her thoughts.

With my restless spirit I tried to take the lead in the emotional boxing ring as I made an attempt to remove my mouth guard. I wanted to ask questions, I needed to be heard. I was unexpectedly silenced for the third time. It was then that I realized that I needed a coach to defend my right to speak.

Pastor Alex explained that I had no reason to hold a grudge against Jack, and there would be no need for counseling because my misery was over. Salvation was the healer.

I sat baffled and went over the events that had just occurred. *Did he just say I didn't need counseling to heal? I have just entered into the emotional boxing ring with my spouse for the second time. His stance is equivalent to saying that after a boxing match, a boxer can go immediately back to train at the gym for his next big event, in spite of any injuries.*

I felt traumatized and knew what I needed to do after our pastor left the house. Jack and I needed to discuss his sinful pattern. I checked on the kids to be sure they were still asleep then went to sit down on the bed.

Jack had gotten into the shower and acknowledged me when I walked into the room. Nervous words left his lips before I could confront him with my perspective.

"You can't tell anyone what I'm about to tell you," he said. He shut the water off and cracked the shower door open. His voice echoed within the walls of the shower as he softly spoke. "You must keep it a secret."

He leaned back in and closed the door. Turning the water back on, he raised his voice to be heard over the spray.

"You know the worst part of all of this? I had a guy lined up from work to do a drive-by shooting. The arrangement was to have it take place before your next birthday, while I was at work. I found out that it was cheaper for me to hire a hitman than to pay for child and spousal support after I left you. His asking price was only two hundred dollars to get the job done."

Jack's last words hit the pit of my stomach like toxic chemicals. I sat calmly and listened to each syllable tumble out of his mouth. His confession struck my ears with his final emotional blow and knocked the wind out of me.

Jack stopped for a moment and briefly popped his head out from around the shower wall. Nonchalantly he asked, "Are you okay?"

I nodded my head and stared at the floor. "Yeah," I said quietly. I knew not to overreact or do anything rash.

While Jack's voice faded to background noise, I began to envision the front of the house. The kids' bedrooms faced the street and were separated by the entryway of the front door. I envisioned the bullet holes in the front of the house and where they would've hit if Jack had carried out his plan. I tried to process the uninvited information as I sat in silence over the horror of what I had just heard.

I spouted off a silent prayer to the Lord, "Heavenly Father, which way do we run?"

I was deeply disturbed with an overwhelming sense of urgency to tell somebody about Jack's plan of premeditated murder.

I remained calm until Jack left for work. A few minutes later the pastor's wife, Miss Tammy, walked over to check on me. We stepped outside to discuss the conversation I'd had with Jack.

"The green mission house that belongs to the church is empty," my voice quivered as I looked her in the eyes, pleading. "Can I please move the kids and I over there until I decide what I need to do to keep us safe?"

Miss Tammy shot me a look of disbelief. I gently grabbed her arm and disclosed Jack's secret plan.

"Jack hired a hitman to drive by and shoot us because he didn't want to pay child or spousal support when he left."

"He's a changed man and I don't think you have anything to worry about!" Miss Tammy spoke with unwavering reassurance.

I couldn't believe her response. Had she understood what I'd said? I rephrased my concerns. "Jack's plan was to kill us and I'm scared."

Miss Tammy paused to gather her thoughts before she spoke again, "In Acts Chapter 9, Saul threatened the Christians with murderous threats. While he was on the journey to carry this out, the Lord intervened. Jack's heart has changed just like Saul's, and his plan to hire a hitman has been intervened by the Holy Spirit. You're going to be okay. You don't need to move out of your house and make him earn your trust back. Jack is a new man in Christ."

After a long pause, I asked, "Should I report this to the cops?"

Miss Tammy's eyes widened as she emphasized her answer with a whisper, "No, you don't need to involve the cops in this matter. It will just complicate things and make it worse."

Sparks of Discernment

Reporting Offenses

"Even though I walk through the darkest valley, I will fear no evil, for You are with me; Your rod and Your staff, they comfort me." (Psalm 23:4 NIV).

We can offer victims of abuse comfort and spiritual guidance with the Shepherd's staff, but the rod of correction should be left for law enforcement to handle. All threats should be reported to law enforcement in the event that there are future occurrences that will threaten the safety of you or your children.

EIGHT

RESUSCITATING RELATIONSHIPS

*J*ack seemed so lighthearted and carefree after his conversion. In spite of his behavior modification, I diligently evaluated his actions and waited for him to lose his temper.

I wanted to believe Jack's salvation was authentic but my heart would not allow me to trust him. Based on past experience, I knew that the truth would reveal itself within three months. I waited patiently to see if Jack could pass my test and receive a seal of authenticity from me. In the past, I'd learned to plan my life around Jack's three month behavior cycle, because it was consistent and never a week late. Each cycle always started the same. The first two days began with irrational behavior, then a few days of unreasonable expectations that ended with an explosive and uncontrollable temper. The next few days after Jack's temper settled down, the kids and I would tiptoe around the house and speak in hushed tones. None of us wanted to trigger another moment of rage. Once Jack calmed down, he would always recommit his life to the Lord and promise to read his Bible, become faithful with church attendance, and live a holy life before the Lord. After three weeks of godly living, he would gradually slip back into his angry sinful self, until it was time to restart his behavior cycle.

Jack was discouraged when I questioned where he was, who he was with, and where he had been. I wasn't sure I wanted to work things out with him this time but I knew I didn't have the support I needed to leave him.

I shared the news of Jack's salvation with my parents but left out all the gory details that led up to his conversion. I didn't want to burden them with worry and fear. There were a lot of questions and emotions I tried to untangle by myself. I felt as if my mind was going in circles because I was unable to come up with a reasonable solution or course of action. I began to realize that I needed a second opinion from an outside source, especially since Pastor Alex's advice was so dismissive and unsettling. I asked around, but found no one to confide in who might have a different view.

I felt forgotten and pushed aside as the excitement of Jack's conversion took the stage. My heart was broken and my trust for him was shattered. I was the only one who struggled with sadness, while the church rejoiced over Jack's decision to follow Jesus.

The people in our church were unaware of Jack's counseling sessions with Pastor Donald at the college in Iowa two years before. They had no idea that he had a history littered with numerous affairs, and they had no reason to question his motives for salvation.

How many more times is Jack going to be unfaithful to me? I asked myself. *He has reassured me that he has changed from his old sinful patterns, but I don't know if I should believe him. He has made many confessions of faith in the past. What makes this time any different? Did Jack think that a fresh salvation experience would be a hopeful attempt to salvage his family since I was suspicious about an affair? Or was his salvation authentic?*

Many weeks had passed since Jack's conversion. To my surprise, he exhibited an excessive exuberance, joy, and freedom from his sinful ways. In spite of my doubts, Jack allowed God to work through him.

Petty Officer Jack

Six weeks after Jack's baptism, he expressed how discontent he was with his job in food service. After work each day, he brought home added tension to our already strained marriage.

After complaining about work for a few weeks, late one evening he expressed to me his desire to join the Navy. I was dumbfounded by his idea, because the kids and I would never see him. There hadn't been enough time since his conversion for us to have rebuilt a relationship of love and trust. In addition, I believed that the temptation for Jack to be unfaithful would be too great. We needed to establish positive attitudes and actions toward each other, before he set out to sea. Then I wondered about the possibility that Jack wanted to join the Navy in order to hide his affections for other women, figuring that I would never find out if he followed through with his desires.

The thought of Jack not being around for the children burdened me more than his unfaithfulness, and I fought in their defense. I would not allow him to silence my opinion if it concerned the children, even if it created an uncomfortable atmosphere.

I took my burdens to the Lord, praying for three days and asking Him to give me the right words to say before I confronted Jack.

"Jack, I don't think it's the right time for you to take a job that is going to take you out of the home for six months."

Jack didn't like my perspective. It was tantrum time. "Why is it that whenever I want to do something, you never support me?"

I was quick to answer, "Support you? I have done nothing but support you."

"Bull crap!" Jack sputtered with frustration.

I stood my ground and yelled back for the first time in our marriage. "I have supported you with the multiple moves we've made in the last six and a half years, to four different states. Never once did I tell you no."

I then turned away from Jack's unhappy face and walked into the laundry room, shutting the door behind me.

The eggshell-colored room contained a peaceful and cool ambiance. I tucked my legs under me as I sat down on the carpet. With tears of sorrow, I bowed my head in prayer.

"Lord, I know I was saved when I was eight years old but this experience with Jack has caused me to doubt my own salvation. Because of my hurt and pain, I cannot decipher if my feelings are normal, or if I'm unsaved. I want the pain in my heart to subside and I want Jack to help me raise the kids in a way that pleases You."

I paused and allowed my heart to melt like wax before the

Lord as I thought about the well-being of my children. "Lord, I need You to take control of Jack's desire to join the Navy."

At that moment, I felt all the tension and stress lift off of my shoulders as the peace of the Lord overtook my uneasy soul.

As I prayed, the Lord made me aware that it was my sin of bitterness toward Jack that separated me from God's blessings on my life. I needed to shift my focus. I left my little prayer room and trusted that God's will would prevail.

The skepticism of where Jack was, what he was doing, or who he was with left my thoughts. Instead, my relationship with the Lord consumed me and it resulted in a desire to create a positive atmosphere for our family to enjoy.

A few weeks had passed and the Navy issue was resolved. Jack and I compromised, and he was sworn into the United States Navy to work in the National Guard as a weekend warrior.

Steps to Salvation

On page 81, I make mention of my salvation experience. You are welcome to take a look at the process and make the decision for yourself. May God bless you.

Here are some basic steps on how to follow Christ so that He can guide you on your journey through life, just as He did for me.

1. Admit that you have sinned.

God's Word tells us that, "All have sinned and

fall short of the glory of God." (Romans 3:23 KJV).

2. Humble yourself before the Lord and ask Him to forgive you of your sin.

"If we confess our sins [to Christ] He is faithful and just to forgive us of our sin and purify us from all unrighteousness." (1 John 1:9 NIV).

3. Ask Christ to become a part of your life, to lead, guide and warn you in your day to day living.

Jesus answered, "I am the Way and the Truth and the Life. No one comes to the Father except through Me." (John 14:6 NIV).

"That if you confess with your mouth that Jesus is Lord and believe in your heart, that God raised Him from the dead, you will be saved." (Romans 10:9 NIV).

4. Find a verse to recall when your circumstances cause you to doubt your security in Christ.

"I give them eternal life, and they shall never perish; no one will snatch them out of My hand." (John 10:28 NIV).

5. Get baptized.

Baptism is a step of obedience that takes place

after salvation. It represents the death, burial, and resurrection of Jesus and is a public confession of your decision to follow Jesus.

In the following verse, John the Baptist speaks about Jesus: "I baptize you with water for repentance, but He who is coming after me is mightier than I, whose sandals I am not worthy to carry. He will baptize you with the Holy Spirit and fire." (Matthew 3:11 ESV).

"And when Jesus was baptized, immediately He went up from the water, and behold, the heavens were opened to Him, and He saw the Spirit of God descending like a dove and coming to rest on Him; and behold, a voice from heaven said, 'This is My beloved Son, with whom I am well pleased.' " (Matthew 3:16-17).

6. Listen for The Holy Spirit.

When you need comfort, the Helper (Holy Spirit) is there for you. Jesus said, "But I tell you the truth, it is to your advantage that I go away; for if I do not go away, the Helper will not come to you; but if I go, I will send Him to you." (John 16:7 NASB).

I encourage you to pray and ask God where He would like you to go to church. It will encourage you and give you the energy to get through the trials you are enduring.

Vows Renewed

In the early spring season of 1996, Jack announced his plan to renew our wedding vows. He had already made plans for the big event with Pastor Alex, then informed me that it would take place on the plateau of Lake Meredith, 39 miles outside of Amarillo, Texas.

A couple weeks later, we packed our camping gear and left for the lake. After camp was set up, I walked to the edge of the plateau and stood in silence. I recalled all the stories I'd heard from local townspeople of how the waters below were infested with black moccasin snakes. I had no desire to test their fierceness.

I then turned toward the old, yellow church bus and studied how it had been parked horizontally to the lake, six feet away from the edge of the ravine. I walked up to the bus with caution to be sure Jack wasn't around the corner. I listened to my gut instinct more attentively after learning about his intentions with the hitman, and I didn't trust him. I didn't want to be close to both him and the edge of a cliff. For the second time, I peered down at the lake below. Suddenly, the warm Texas wind pushed up against my body as a sense of danger washed over me.

I cautioned myself not to get any closer to the ravine, then double checked my surroundings to be sure Jack was nowhere to be found. When I turned, I found his eyes on me and worried that he wished to charge me like a bull and push me over the berm. After Jack made eye contact with me, he quickly turned away to talk to the pastor.

I walked back to camp to freshen up and prepare for the

renewal of the vows. Miss Tammy gleefully followed me into the tent, then grabbed my hands in delight. As she turned me to face her, she asked, "Isn't this exciting?"

"I guess," I responded with doubt and disappointment. "Jack never asked me if I wanted to do this."

Miss Tammy gently let go of my hands and quietly left the tent.

I stood alone and powdered my nose and rearranged my hair, after the wind had had its way with it. My thoughts began to drown out any concerns over my appearance. *Why am I doing this? I think I'm still in shock over Jack's desire to kill the kids and me.*

My thoughts quickly turned into a rant and then into a series of questions. *Jack never asked me to remarry him. Now that I think of it, during our college years he never asked me to be his girlfriend either. A few months after that, he told me that we were going to get married. Why couldn't I see his deceptive strategy to dodge any chance of rejection from me? Why am I afraid to voice my opinion to Jack? Who tries to kill their family and gets away with it? What kind of monster did I marry? Why does he expect me to move forward in this relationship with forgiveness, and why does he feel that it is an injustice for me to feel any hurt or betrayal from the deceit of his actions? Is it because he doesn't respect women and he doesn't see me as his equal?*

Since the time of Jack's conversion, he seemed to consistently schedule events that centered around himself. First it was his baptism, then his testimony. After that, we spent weeks on the Navy issue, and now it was the renewal of our vows. Each event gave me little time to work through the hurt of his unfaithfulness. I felt as if he were pushing me to live my life in fast forward motion, when I actually just needed him to push the pause button. I needed a slower pace and some space to process all the bottled up pain I felt from the last six years of our marriage. I forgave Jack and I was no longer bitter. Nevertheless, I had many issues to overcome because I was still deeply hurt and still feared for my life.

I took a deep breath, put on my happy face, and tried to leave my negative thoughts in the tent. In my hand-me-down jeans and torn shirt, I walked out to the front of the crowd where I joined hands with Jack, who wore a nice pair of jeans with a new shirt and boots. Obediently, I recited my vows while doubt and fear continued to brew within.

Sparks of Discernment

Truck Check and RIP

Every month at the fire station, we had meetings that included truck checks. We needed to make sure that the trucks were ready to go so that we could arrive at the scene of an emergency with efficiency.

A few things that truck checks included were inventory of all needed supplies, making sure all equipment was organized and placed in the designated area, and ensuring that everything was in working order.

In a home where abuse exists, it's important that you do your own checks:

1. Take inventory on the emotional state of each family member and communicate observations to a doctor, counselor, and a supportive pastor.

2. Make sure bags are packed with food, money, water, diapers, baby formula, a bottle, an extra pacifier, and at least a change of clothes, in case an emergency exit becomes necessary. Kids need security. Make a mental note of that special blanket, doll or truck, they would want to take with them. Because the abuser may find the bag and it may cause conflict, I would advise you to keep it at the house of a trusted friend.

3. Keep phones charged and medications in a basket placed in a spot where it would be easy to grab and go. Always have a list of phone numbers of people you trust with you at all times. Be ready to calmly call 911 with the information that they would need to assist you, such as your address and nearby street names or landmarks.

4. Keep calm. If you are unable to retrieve all

the items you need, you can ask the police to assist you for a quick sweep through the house. If you need to go back to your home, leave the kids with a friend to create less confusion for them. Keep in mind that because the kids have seen and heard enough abuse already, you will want to minimize their trauma as much as possible. Do your best to keep them away from heated conversations and situations.

Your RIP goes hand in hand with your truck check. RIP stands for Rapid Intervention Procedure. The RIP fire team is always on standby, geared up and ready to intervene in case there is a firefighter down. Once we are called in, we grab an emergency tank filled with oxygen, in case the injured firefighter's tank is on empty.

In an abusive situation, you must mentally prepare yourself for an emergency exit so you don't lose a member of your family. When the abuser is nowhere around, and without causing confusion to the kids, practice your Rapid Intervention Procedures. Think of different exits that you and the kids can take out of the house. Plan out multiple routes to the houses of trusted friends or family members, and know the location and route to your local police department.

"Guard me as You guard Your own eyes; hide me in the shadow of Your wings." **Psalm 17:8 NLT**

NINE

CLIFF RESCUE

*T*here was a major shift that took place in our lives due to Jack's salvation experience, and it was a stark contrast to how things had gone up to that point. I no longer had to worry about his fits of rage or how he treated the children when I wasn't around. Our time was now spent with positive experiences, as we took a vacation from all of our past sorrows.

We explored Palo Duro Canyon in Canyon, Texas and awed at the colors and unique geological formations of the Spanish Skirts. We hiked the trail that led to Lighthouse Rock and then walked up a stone trail that led to a washed out cave of sandstone. The cave was cool and the quarters were tight, but we managed to get everybody inside to carve our names on the wall.

To cool off from our trail experience, I took the boys' shoes off and waded with them in the Prairie Dog Town Fork Red River, until they sank down to their knees in the murky red clay. I told them about the natives who lived in the canyon many years ago and how they used the river water to cook and clean. I took advantage of the teachable moment, loving the opportunity to turn the trip into a history lesson. I thought about the verse,

"Remember My words with your whole being. Write them down and tie them to your hands as a sign: tie them on your foreheads to remind you. Teach them well to your children, talking about them when you sit at home and walk along the road, when you lie down and when you get up. Write them on your doors and gates so that both you and your children will live a long time in the land." (Deuteronomy 11:18-21).

Because of Jack's patterns, I knew I would face many unexpected challenges in life and I was sure that if I homeschooled I could carry out the commands in Deuteronomy 11. Frequent moves can cause many setbacks in school-aged children, and I was afraid that our frequent moving would cause my kids' education to suffer. I could see that the setbacks in their education could too easily become our focus instead of God's word. So as we washed our feet in the river, I made a commitment to God to teach my children to walk in the ways of the Lord, for I knew that it may be the only inheritance I would get to pass down to them.

The last trip we took in the wild West was with Jack's parents. We went sightseeing at the top of a plateau with a magnificent view. Before it was time to leave, I wanted to get one last look at the incredible beauty stretching out all around us. Jack agreed to watch the kids while I wandered around. Standing at the edge of a steep cliff to look down, I estimated that the tops of the trees were at least 110 stories below my feet.

I turned around to see where my family was and the blood in my veins turned cold. Jack had the kids posed for a photo, three steps away from the edge of the ravine. Peter stood in front of an old piece of driftwood. Josiah reached up and wrapped his tiny hands around a branch of an old tree, and Samantha sat on a stump. I yelled at Jack in horror, "What are you doing? That's a dangerous drop off!"

I couldn't run toward the kids fast enough. Jack merely smiled back and quickly took a few steps away from the children to snap a picture. "I got the picture and it's not so dangerous."

Just then, Josiah's arms gave out and he let go of the branch. He stumbled and lost his balance on the uneven terrain.

I screamed as I watched my four-year-old son slide down the sharply-angled ravine. The sound of his little body being carried away on pebbles horrified me. By God's holy grace of preservation, there was one little sapling embedded into the side of the hill. It stood about two feet tall and was about two inches in diameter. Little Josiah grabbed on and held tight with both hands as he screamed out in terror, begging for help.

Jack commanded me to run and get his father, who was parked six yards away. As Wayne ran toward Josiah, he ordered Jack to lie flat on the ground to form a human chain. Jack crawled down the side of the cliff on his belly to grab Josiah, while Wayne held Jack's feet. I watched Jack's head disappear over the edge, followed by his upper body, then his hips and thighs. Now all that remained at the top of the plateau was a portion of Jack's calves and his feet.

The rescue was a success but left us all shaken. I was furious that Jack dared to put our children in such a dangerous position, but at the same time I was grateful that he had the guts to rescue our son from disaster.

We all sat in shock once we were back in the van. We tried to put the accident behind us and never bothered to discuss what had transpired. After Josiah's cliff incident, I decided that I no longer needed to experience the adventures of the wild West.

When we arrived back home in Amarillo, I thought of activities we could do together that weren't so dangerous. We slid down grassy hills on broken down cardboard boxes and rode down the gullies during heavy rains. We reminisced about our adventures and unusual sightings in Texas as we drank hot chocolate and watched the light show in the sky that each thunderstorm brought.

During one particular storm when we lived in the trailer, we were warned to find shelter. We drove out of the twelve mile path of an F2 tornado, just in time to feel the strength of its pull on the back end of our car. The tornado changed direction at the last minute and allowed us to escape its destructive effects.

We saw baseball-sized hail and the damage it caused to local car dealerships. We also witnessed dirt devils and sand storms. They all sound miserable and scary, but each discovery brought our family amazement and wonder.

Through all of our family adventures, Jack became a family man. The connection was real and his salvation experience proved to be authentic.

Meltdown

In spite of the newfound joy our family discovered together, I struggled to heal from the hurt of Jack's immorality and as a result, insecurity plagued my soul. I was sure Jack's salvation was genuine until I discovered that he had rehired the same hitman a second time. He would have followed through with killing me if I had chosen to report Jack's first offense of attempted murder.

I didn't know what to think of this new information, especially since Jack had been so nice to me. The only people I trusted were my parents, and at this point in my life I desperately needed their wisdom and support.

Jack was tired of his job, so I took the opportunity to ask if we could move to my hometown in Michigan. Jack was all for the move, and I was elated that I would get what I asked for.

Jack was honorably discharged from the National Guard because of our move north. I was surprised that he gave it up, since he had put up such a fight to join.

We were officially on our fourteenth move, during Memorial Day weekend in 1997. Jack placed Peter and Josiah in the moving truck with him, and Samantha sat with me in the front seat of our car, which we affectionately referred to as the Old Grey Hare. I had no doubt that the Old Grey Hare would make the trip to Michigan. However, I wasn't so sure about Jack's decision to put our twenty-pound dog, Lady, and her new litter of puppies on the floor of the back seat.

Jack walked over to my side of the car and handed me a walkie-talkie through the car window. He gave me a demonstration on how to use it, then warned me that they would only work within a certain range of each other. The only bad thing was, Jack wanted to save the battery power and told me to turn it on only in a moment of distress.

We traveled north until we hit rush hour traffic in Nebraska. The traffic was fast and I was uncomfortable with the unfamiliar area and terrain. I felt more collected when I drove on two-lane country roads that were only overcrowded by large farm equipment and milk trucks.

The crazy four-lane expressway, with on-ramps and exits everywhere, frightened me. I felt an element of surprise rush over me when I realized our exit was up ahead. Jack had refused to tell me which exit I needed ahead of time, instead commanding, "Just keep your eyes on the back of the moving truck."

That plan failed when four semi-trucks blocked my view and boxed me in. I couldn't see ahead of me from one exit to the next.

I frantically grabbed my walkie-talkie and spoke, "Jack? Jack, I know you can hear me. Pick up your radio and talk to me. I can't see you! Just give me the exit number!"

Jack wouldn't answer. I found myself screaming his name into the device.

"Jaaaaack!"

I let out a growl of disbelief, "I can't believe this! We are going to be separated forever and I will never get to see my boys again!"

Samantha sat in silence as she watched me have a meltdown. I paused, realizing she had never seen me act this way before. I knew that my actions were providing her with enough entertainment to reenact in a theater someday. As I paused, I heard my inner voice say, *Look at what you're doing.*

Overwhelmed and frantic, I yelled out with a raspy voice, "I can't look, there's too much traffic!"

The Holy Spirit moved within me and caused my eyes to look down at the walkie-talkie. I had it upside down, backwards and the switch was turned off. I rolled my eyes out of frustration, turned the walkie-talkie right side up, and switched it on. Just then the semi that had blocked me from behind left the expressway. I let off the gas to allow the other semi-trucks to move ahead of me. Unfortunately, I was still sandwiched in amongst nonstop traffic, the pace of which kept my heart racing. Finally, Jack answered me.

"This is our exit."

I spotted his truck twenty-five yards ahead of me on the off ramp. I still had time to move out of the middle lane to follow him. Gratefully, I left the chaos of Nebraska behind, feeling instead the anticipation of reuniting with my boys again.

We met up at a restaurant in Iowa to stretch our legs and get a bite to eat. Nobody was hungry and it was a good thing. We were served pasty potatoes from a box, which surprised me since Idaho was only four states away. Peter and Josiah tried their meatloaf and immediately spit it out. The meat was chewy and had probably just come out of the microwave. After we tried to eat, we loaded up in the vehicles and drove straight through Iowa and on to Chicago.

Little Black Bag

My mind drifted and I began to think about how nice it would be to stop for a short nap. My thoughts were interrupted as I pulled up to the attendant at the toll booth for the Chicago turnpike. I put my car in park then realized that I hadn't been given any money for the trip. I turned on my walkie-talkie and yelled for Jack. He didn't answer, so I waved my radio out the car window with the hope that he would see me in his side mirror. He had already paid his toll fee, then pulled ahead forty yards to wait for me.

The longer I waited for him to respond, the more I began to fume. As time progressed, I realized that he probably couldn't see me, so I put the radio up higher and frantically waved it outside my car window. The toll booth attendant caught the corner of my eye. I turned my head in her direction to notice that she had stepped away from the window, presumably out of concern for her safety.

"Ma'am," I addressed her apologetically and as kindly as I could in the midst of my frustration. "He left me with no money, I am so sorry!"

She moved forward a step, shrugged her shoulders and answered, "Hey honey, do what you have to."

Just then I heard Jack's voice come over the radio. "What's your problem?" he barked. "Calm down!"

He had hit my last nerve, so I yelled back, "You left me with no money to pay the toll fee and then drove off!"

"Settle down, I have it covered!" Jack's voice was infuriatingly calm. "Look for a little black velvet bag in one of the suitcases."

"Which suitcase did you put the tiny black bag in?"

"I don't know," came the answer.

I looked up at the toll booth collector and apologized again for taking so long. Putting the radio down, I paused and took a deep breath, then surveyed the mountain of suitcases that were stacked up in the backseat. I prayed, "Lord, which one is it in?"

I realized that the Lord was probably amused over my dilemma after I looked through suitcase number two. I dug frantically through each suitcase, leaving the contents all over the back seat. I was at the pinnacle of my anxiety and worried that I would melt down in tears if a car dared to pull up behind me and honk its horn.

Samantha sat quietly with amusement as she watched the drama unfold. Lady gave a look of concern as she hovered over her pups on the floor of the back seat.

"I'm sorry, Lady," I soothed. "I won't hurt you or your puppies."

I opened the last of the seven suitcases and pulled out my tiny bag of treasure. I poured all the change into my hand and discovered that I had exactly what I needed for the toll fee, without a penny to spare.

We drove onto the turnpike and were officially Michigan-bound. The rest of the drive gave me plenty of time to think about how much control Jack had over our finances. What if I had been separated from Jack on the expressway? I had no money to feed Samantha or to make a phone call and we would have been forced to sleep in the car. *Why is it that Jack never gives me any extra money?*

I trusted Jack with the finances, but this trip helped me to see how dependent on him I was, and how unhealthy it was for him to have so much control.

TEN

OVERCAST WITH DISCOURAGEMENT

Once we crossed the Michigan border, I left my thoughts of co-dependency behind me. I was excited to be in my home state near my family, as I hadn't seen them in over four years.

They were happy to see us and kind enough to pay our bills for the next three months. To my surprise and embarrassment, Jack refused to find work, so I took a part-time job at a local grocery store.

In the meantime, Jack looked for more animals to add to our homestead. His new stress-free lifestyle led him on quests for guinea pigs, turtles, and other aquatic creatures for the kids to enjoy. He pushed my patience too far when he brought home a big, beautiful, black lab for Peter. I was ashamed that Jack expected my parents to pay for the increased supply of pet food. However, there was no way I was going to be the bad guy and take Peter's new friend away from him.

After being out of work for three months, Jack finally received the phone call he had been holding out for. My uncle Matt hired him to be a delivery driver for his electric company. Once Jack began to work, his tension and tendencies for control returned.

A few weeks later, Jack added another animal to our pet farm. Samantha made claims on the white cat and named him Johnny Rocket. Johnny's superpower was to eat giant blue bottle flies. He would jump up in mid-air to catch one in his mouth and then shake off the buzz with a quick swallow. I discovered that Josiah liked to stuff Johnny into his pillowcase and swing him around in circles before shooting foam discs at him. Josiah received a lot of guidance from me on how to treat a pet, and gradually learned to be gentle.

I loved when the brisk smell of the Michigan air beckoned my children to play outside. The boys would paint Native American symbols on old blankets, then prop them up with sticks around the apple trees to make teepees. I watched as they played, and noticed that they acted differently without Jack around. When Jack was at work, joy filled our home. When he came home, stress and tension filled the air.

I escaped from those thoughts as Samantha giggled and bounced by me in her butterfly costume. She was free, we were all free from Jack's oppressive nature. The happiness resounded within each of us and carried a peaceful note throughout the day.

The strain of the winter season affected Jack's demeanor and it caused him to take his frustrations out on me. He battled internal temptations throughout the day and by evening he was worn out from the struggle. He claimed he loved me, but his anger was greater than his love and it caused me to cry in silence.

In the evening while I cleaned up, I studied the starlit sky from my tiny kitchen window. I would look down the street to see who else was home and wondered if their families struggled as much as ours did.

I felt responsible for Jack's emotional state and did what I could to make his life easier. I took care of all the yard and home responsibilities. My desire was to create an environment of peace, but instead it gave Jack more ammunition to snap at me. My only escape from Jack's oppression was prayer. I trusted God with my requests and He always gave me what I needed, as evidenced by Jack staying outside to shovel snow after work each night. I was grateful to learn that he'd made a commitment to pray and let all his aggression out before he walked in the door to greet the family.

Church Life

Once we settled in, we began attending the church that I had gone to in my youth. I was grateful to the church leaders when I saw their efforts to help Jack mature, urging him forward on his spiritual path with encouragement. Eventually he was given the chance to teach a Sunday school class.

Jack looked nice and felt secure when he wore his long duster jacket, like the ones worn in old Western movies. He set it off nicely with a bolo tie, leather cowboy boots, and a cowboy hat. The western motif gave him a sense of confidence and he used that sureness to challenge the church congregation with new ideas for church growth. While he did have a successful formula for growth, he did not know how to share it with a heart of mercy. Instead, he was combative, and hurt many of our friends and family. I wanted to run and hide from all the humiliation he caused me.

Summer

In the year 1999, we approached our second summer in northern Michigan. I was glad when the winter weather was pushed away with warm air. I had some fun things in mind for the kids to do that summer that I had enjoyed as a child.

We rode our bikes around town and always made sure to speed past the large herd of cows that grazed in a nearby pasture. We could feel the thunder of their steps as they ran toward the fence with their wide, wild eyes to watch us whiz by. The kids would burst out with laughter as they greeted the cows and begged to repeat the same route over and over again.

Jack surprised me with his social skills that summer when he gleefully participated in the town's summer festivities. He helped the kids decorate their bikes for the parade and walked around town with a friendly wave and smile. Peter won three different raffle drawings that day and came home with a new fishing pole, a bike, and a remote control car. Samantha won first place in the bike parade as Mother Goose, and Josiah won the hearts of the town folk with his funny antics.

The kids and I were refreshed with Jack's energetic spirit. Excitement always prevailed when we would drive north to view the lighthouses and watch the large sailboats float by on Lake Michigan. We visited picturesque towns like Charlevoix, Petoskey,

Ludington, and Traverse City. In each town we would search for Petoskey stones and play with the crayfish that crawled along the rocks on the shoreline. During lunch we shared our food with the seagulls, while we buried our toes in the soft, warm, summer sand.

The kids and I always looked forward to the periods during which the rough waves of Jack's emotional storms would subside. The reward seemed so sweet and left us longing for more, for we enjoyed our time together.

The New Church

Jack was encouraged when our church hired a pastor with the same leadership style that he had. However, the congregation did not respond well to the new pastor. Once Jack heard about this disapproval, he decided to break off from the church I grew up in to start a new place of worship. While we searched for a head pastor to lead the new church, Jack took on the duty of delivering the Sunday sermons. I became concerned when Jack fell to his knees in the middle of his first sermon. He looked up to heaven and cried out, "Lord, forgive me for being like Paul, who also was a murderer."

Jack's confession left me in a daze and I wondered if what I heard was true. I looked around at the small crowd of people to see if anybody else seemed as concerned as I was.

Once we arrived home, I pulled Jack into the bedroom and shut the door. Jack sat on the corner of the bed and asked, "What did you think of the message?"

"The message was good, Jack," I answered, contemplating how to broach the subject that had me on edge.

He sat with anticipation and waited for more praise. I repeated, more loudly, "You did good, Jack!"

"I didn't say too much did I?" he asked.

"What do you mean?"

"I didn't give away too much about my past, did I?"

I remained calm, and attempted to cleverly pry for a full confession, with intentions to file a police report.

"Jack, what did you mean when you fell to your knees and asked the Lord to forgive you for being like Paul, who also was a murderer?"

Jack's eyes grew large and he remained still, like a deer that had been spotted. He slowly lifted his body off the bed and backed away from me with caution.

"Have you been involved with a murder?" I asked.

Jack shook his head back and forth to say no. I wasn't at peace with the way he responded to my question, and it left me leery of his trustworthiness.

Sparks of Discernment

Elements of Ignition

A fire needs three elements to exist: oxygen, heat, and fuel. For example, when there are flames inside a brick oven it is evidence there is heat, a fuel source, and some oxygen.

Three elements an abuser needs to ignite their rage are victims, a disagreeable problem, and anger. If you take away one of those elements (such as you and the kids) it will snuff out the anger.

A victim of abuse is empowered when he or she stands up for themselves. However, you should be aware that the situation could turn violent because an abuser often interprets you voicing your opinion as an act of disrespect toward their authority and it could kindle the abuser's anger and cause it to heat up faster.

This is not a justification or encouragement to keep quiet, but rather a point of reference and warning to better prepare you for possible dangerous outcomes.

ELEVEN

WEATHER ADVISORY

- - - - - - - - - - - - - - -

TRIGGER WARNING

TRIGGER WARNING to reader: this section contains animal cruelty. If you choose to avoid this section to protect your emotional and mental well-being, please skip ahead to A New Start on page 120.

- - - - - - - - - - - - - - -

$\mathcal{I}$n 1998, Jack applied for a job forty-five minutes north, not too far from Traverse City, Michigan. He was hired with more pay than he'd made at his previous job, and was offered a nice benefit package.

I had three weeks to pack for another move. To complicate matters, I couldn't find a house to rent that would accept our tiny pet farm. I had to put my heart in a drawer and give each pet away except the fly-eating cat, Johnny Rocket and Chase, Peter's best friend.

A few days before our move north, Jack told us to wait for him in the car. After ten minutes had passed, I became concerned and thought I should check on him. I glanced back at the kids and told them to stay put while I went to assess the situation.

I opened the garage door and stood in shock and sorrow at the scene before me. Jack held Chase's limp head in his hand. On the ground was a pool of blood that trailed out of the pup's mouth. Silence and hurt was all that I could express with my body language. Jack had punched the dog in the head to its death. He again exhibited the same smile of satisfaction and peace he had when he killed my cat in 1991. I left the garage brokenhearted and disturbed. When I walked back to the car, I thought about how Jack had claimed to leave his old ways behind, after he received Jesus as his Savior.

Peter noticed that something wasn't sitting right with me. "Mom, what's wrong? Is everything okay?" he asked.

I couldn't hold his gaze as I searched for the right thing to say. "Yeah, I guess."

I held my tongue. Peter was too young to feel the disappointment of betrayal. I needed to protect his emotions and innocence. So far, I felt that I had been successful at keeping my children tightly under my wing, sheltered from Jack's rage, mood swings, and abusive behavior. But kids are perceptive. I was starting to wonder about the effects that Jack's impulsive and unhealthy habits might have on my children.

Jack came out from the garage carefree and whimsical. Peter studied his dad, then studied my reaction. He didn't ask any more questions but his mind was curious.

Once we arrived back home from that day's outing, Jack made sure the garage was locked so the kids wouldn't see Chase and the blood. He then walked into the house to make an announcement. "Chase ran away."

Peter's eyes filled with sadness as Jack explained that it was probably best, since we couldn't find a home for him. Jack continued, "Somebody will find him and see how sweet he is, and they will want to keep him."

A New Start

We made the move north, near Traverse City, walking away from the new church that Jack had started.

Once we felt settled, we joined a homeschool group for guidance in our educational endeavors. The kids needed an outlet from family life and loved the activities the group offered. In the process, we became good friends with Don and Amanda. They mentored Jack and me, and taught us how to teach according to each child's learning style. They also showed us how to turn our day trips into educational experiences.

We walked the Skegemog Trails to sketch the landscape and create poems to match our observations. We hiked the Boardman River trails and felt the anticipation of danger as we spotted fresh bear tracks in the shimmery, white snow. We experienced the ambiance of peacefulness as we watched the mighty kingfisher gracefully float through the sky and swoop down to dive for fish.

I was pleased that Jack was in tune with the emotional and educational needs of our children. The power of the spiritual influence and support he received from other homeschool dads was noticeable, but he still secretly struggled with his cycle of emotional turmoil.

The following year, my doctor informed me that our immune systems were compromised due to stress. The only thing I could link it to was Jack's unpredictable moods and how it created upheaval for the kids and me. The kids suffered from chronic strep throat and developed allergies that led to asthma and eczema. I suffered from large quantities of hair loss and constant upper respiratory infections, along with a sensitivity toward household chemicals. I could no longer handle antibiotics and had to switch to homeopathic methods to allow my body to heal from infections.

I was unable to verbally express the unhealthy challenges Jack brought to my life. I knew that if I did, he would accuse me of being a backstabber and might then retaliate. I needed advice but instead I chose to suffer in silence. I stuffed all my secrets in a locked trunk in the corner of my soul. I felt it was best to leave the trunk hidden. I knew that if I opened it, I would suffer a lifetime of silent treatments and constant emotional turmoil.

I coped with my frustrations through prayer. I also had a system of writing things down in an attempt to sort through the chaos. I would make two separate columns on a sheet of paper. In the first column I wrote down all the qualities I appreciated about Jack. In the second column I wrote down all the frustrations and disappointments he brought to my life. I filled half the page with all the good qualities of our relationship, but ran out of space when I wrote down all the things that frustrated me.

My problem was always the same. I chose to focus on all the positive qualities of my relationship with Jack, attempting to ignore the issues that brought stress. Eventually, it all compiled into a large knot of confusion that created more health issues for me later in life.

Sparks of Discernment

Stress and Illness

Dr. Robert M. Sapolsky is a professor of biology and neurology. In his book, *Why Zebras Don't Get Ulcers*, he explains that zebras don't suffer from stress-related illnesses because their stress is fleeting. A zebra might endure being chased by a predator but after the chase is over, it has time to recover.

In my experience, the stress that victims of abuse endure is constant, even if they take time to get away. You may go on vacation or have a girls' day out, but you always find yourself making decisions based on how you know your abuser will react if he disapproves of a decision you've made.

The truth is, a victim of abuse may never be free from their oppressor's reaction. And the stress and emotional abuse they encounter could be more constant than they have ever dared to evaluate.

Sapolsky explains how constant stress weakens the physiology of the body. For example, the stress I endured caused memory loss, digestive problems, low blood sugar, complications with hand-eye coordination, heightened sensitivity to loud and sudden noises, and problem-solving issues.

The longer a victim of abuse goes without intervention, it becomes more likely that their chances for developing more physiological problems will increase.

"The righteous person may have troubles, but the Lord delivers him from them all." (Psalm 34:19).

God is good on His Word. I have been delivered from most of the physiological symptoms from the years of abuse I endured. But it has taken a lot of effort on my part to seek out ways to retrain my brain and my body's responses to stress.

Spiritual Goggles

When the boys were seven and eight years old, Jack thought it would be fun to play a war board game with them.

I watched with gleeful anticipation as the excitement grew around the table. I grabbed a video camera to capture the moment. They pulled the game out of the box and began to play. Once a few minutes had passed, my perspective began to shift. It was as if I had spiritual goggles on. For the first time, I was able to interpret Jack's interaction with the boys from a different point of view.

I came to the realization that Jack never allowed the kids to joke around or actually have fun when we played games. His rigid style of game play created tension for everybody involved, as he overpowered and controlled each scenario in the game.

I was taught that a game was a tool used for bonding and creating fun quality time with the family. Jack, on the other hand, used it to assert his authority and control, as he micromanaged where the boys placed their tiny plastic game pieces on the board. Jack made it appear as if it were a life-threatening job, not a joy.

I struggled with what I saw, and realized that our normal was not a healthy normal.

Ministry

We settled on a church located on the outskirts of Traverse City. One particular couple we met was Thad and Ann, who had a Boston terrier named Rugby. The kids adored her. Ann and I spent a few afternoons together without the guys, and while the children played with Rugby, Ann and I shared many deep secrets. Because she was easy for me to talk to, I told her how Jack had planned to hire a hitman to kill the kids and me. I had to stop in the middle of the story to calm my nerves, before continuing on and wrapping it up with how Jack's salvation proved to be God's intervention.

Ann's face turned white as a sense of uneasiness overtook her spirit. She asked with a nervous voice, "And you're still with him?"

Instantly I began to rethink the theories I had been forced to accept from the Texas pastor and his wife. Maybe I should have left Jack after all. I thought I was the only one who thought that Jack's idea to hire a hitman was unacceptable and should have been handled differently.

Ann's negative reaction to the news left me worried. I became scared that Jack would find out what I told Ann. I let a few days pass before I cleared my conscience by telling Jack about our conversation. After that, he began to look for a reason to leave the little country church and started to pull away from all the solid friendships we'd made.

We ended up in a different church that was in search of a new pastor. We connected the congregation to the pastor from my hometown. The church hired him, and Jack took over the music and youth ministries.

The ministry team and church leaders all agreed on a shared vision for the church and it resulted in rapid growth. Jack was encouraged with what he saw and it put a positive spin on the way he viewed life. He was suddenly fun and charismatic to be around all the time.

Jack tried to create a family atmosphere for the teens who struggled with their purpose in life. He gave them direction and hope. The teens were serious about their relationships with the

Lord and many were saved and baptized under Jack's teaching.

In the meantime, I became good friends with the director of the children's ministry, Mrs. Wright.

One morning, I looked through my email and noticed that she had sent me a note. I was excited to hear what she planned for the kids to do that month. I quickly realized that the email was not about the children's ministry at all, but it was meant to inform me of her views that Jack was abusive. I was appalled that Mrs. Wright had the audacity to think he was abusive, since he never hit me. I was so upset over the letter that I let go of my relationship with Mrs. Wright.

Sparks of Discernment

Breathing House

One thing firefighters must observe when they arrive on the scene of a fire is the state of the windows. They must take note of any windows that have a build-up of soot on them, and note if the house is breathing.

Sometimes when there is a house fire, gases will build, and puffs of smoke will breathe out from the cracks of the house. When this happens, it is a warning sign that an explosion could happen at any moment.

Oftentimes, neighbors, relatives, or friends are aware that a house on their block is breathing with abuse. Sometimes the abuser will yell loudly enough for neighbors to hear the explosive behavior taking place.

Do your neighbor a favor and save the wife (or husband) and kids from further abuse by calling 911 during their distress. They may be in a position in which they are unable to get to the phone. Rapid intervention can happen if you make the call so that police can intervene in a dangerous situation. They can help to cool down a bad temper before the breathing house explodes into something even worse. If the warning signs do not seem to indicate an immediate emergency but do indicate potential danger, offer to go with the victim to speak with a counselor and/or authorities.

TWELVE

EYE OF THE STORM

*J*ack loved his new job that had brought us further north, and I was happy that he received regular pay raises. For the first time in our married life, we didn't have to depend on the state to pay for our food.

In 2002, Jack decided to buy a house. I was elated because it meant stability for the kids and freedom to have a garden. We settled on a home in Grawn, Michigan. I was pleased that it sat next to a wooded area that offered many nature hikes for the kids and me to explore. The kids would also have endless opportunities to make new friends, and a chance to create good childhood memories.

I was committed to my marriage with Jack, in spite of how he treated me. I felt that home ownership was my reward for what I had endured in our marriage. Our home of 1,200 square feet felt like a mansion compared to the two-bedroom trailers and apartments we'd previously dwelt in.

I loved the fresh smell of pine in the air, the dirt beneath my feet, and the view our little town offered with its eighty-foot pine trees. They were beautifully decorated with large snow caps in the winter months, which created a lovely ambiance for the Christmas season.

The summer months were filled with many activities. We often drove a few miles down the road to swim in the Betsie River. The kids would hold their breath, then dive off a large pipe that stuck out from under the bridge. The undercurrent of the river would push them to the top of the water and carry them toward the edge of the man-made dam of large logs.

On the weekends we planted flowers and walked through the woods to investigate birds, plants, trees, mushrooms, and animal tracks. Our favorite thing was to observe the wildlife that would visit our bird feeders. We had raccoon, possum, turkey, and even an albino squirrel. There were many species of birds, but the largest were the pileated woodpeckers. When they approached the feeders, the kids and I would stop whatever we were doing and slowly crawl on the living room floor toward the large picture window. Our goal was to get as close to the window as we could, without being seen by the two-and-a-half-foot birds. Our laughter forced the game to be over when the woodpeckers would land on the suet feeders, swinging freely as they obliterated the suet cakes with their powerful, sharp beaks.

On the warmer weekends we set up camp in the backyard and cooked our meals over the campfire with the tripod that Peter and Josiah built. Jack was always the first one up in the morning. He was happy to cook hot cakes on an iron skillet over the open fire. The smell of the smoky-flavored cakes would drift into our tents, beckoning us to come out to eat.

We played card games in the evening, and when the sun went down, we played Surviving The Land Of Dog Poo. The goal was to keep our shoes clean while we ran an obstacle course. When a player had poo on the shoe they were out of the game until voted back in at the next meeting.

The kids raised three ducks, naming them Coco, Colo and Aflek. They would herd them around the backyard as if they were sheep.

We had fun, and wanted to share our joy with a foster child. We applied for the position and were approved. Enough time had passed since Jack's major behavioral issues that no one could have picked up on the discord that he had regularly brought into the home before. Jack had compassion for the foster kids and it seemed to give him a new purpose. He was able to use the abuse he'd experienced as a child to redirect the foster children on a positive path. Our home became a place of peace, and the foster children never witnessed any of the rage or abuse Jack had previously been prone to.

Because we owned our home, Jack had a reason to appreciate his job and grew content with the lifestyle that consisted of steady, stable work. He embraced country life and was able to relax in the fresh country air.

Our lives had finally seemed to straighten out from all the trials, tribulations, and tension we had endured. Life was now full of bubbles, candy, and everything nice. I was so excited to see the clouds lifting. The sun was breaking through, and bringing with it our happily ever after.

I could tell you what many of you are expecting to hear. That Jack is now a changed man and all the prayers, worry, and hurt are a thing of the past. That he is no longer emotionally abusive. But through the years I have learned that abusive behaviors and tendencies don't disappear just because of one's faith in Jesus Christ. An abuser must commit their issues to an experienced counselor for many years, to retrain the way they cope and deal with other people. The abusive tendencies are ingrained into the way they think and it is natural for them to relate to others in this unhealthy manner.

Encounter

I was working two afternoons a week for another homeschool mom in her downstairs office. She also employed a few other moms from the community. The opportunity gave the kids a chance to socialize with other homeschoolers and gave me a chance to make new friends as well.

Though our family had gone through a period of smooth sailing, it gradually became apparent that my standards for respectful treatment and healthy relationships had been significantly lowered. Slowly but surely, Jack's controlling nature crept back to the forefront. And slowly but surely, I began to walk on eggshells again.

Jack had approved of my decision to work once he knew that I would be home in time to greet him when he came home from work. Jack seemed to demand more family time as the kids grew older. He also became more possessive and enforced time restraints when we visited family and friends. He would get angry and jealous if we were out longer than the time he allotted.

One afternoon, while I was at work, all five of us moms had a deep conversation about what God was doing in our lives. Then all of them turned toward me at once and asked if they could pray over me. Nobody had ever done that for me before, and the idea of all that attention made me uncomfortable, but I consented. At that time I didn't fully understand what took place that day, but they had planted a seed that began to open my eyes. Because of their prayer over me, the events that happened over the course of the next three years with Jack made me more and more aware of his emotionally abusive tendencies.

Jack and I joined a small group at church, where we met Elizabeth and Rod. Our group grew close spiritually, because we all felt comfortable enough to share our personal stories of how God took our hurts and sorrows and made them into something beautiful.

The members of our small group had the opportunity to attend a weekend retreat put on by DeColores Ministries, the focus of which was spiritual connection, fellowship, and renewal. Jack attended the men's retreat one weekend, and I was able to go to the women's retreat the next weekend without any resistance from him. The idea of the weekend scared me because I would be away from him for three days, without any contact. He had conditioned me to believe that my primary responsibility was to be available for his beck and call, and I was unsure how he would emotionally hold up without me. Partially because I wasn't sure how he would do, and partly out of concern for the kids, I arranged for Elizabeth's husband, Rod, and the pastor of our church to check in with Jack while I was away.

All the women gathered together in the sanctuary on the

first night to listen to the speaker, then we broke off into prayer groups. After that, I went back to my room where I found a large grocery sack filled with gifts, each with a small note attached to it. I poured the gifts out onto my sleeping bag and spent the next three hours in tears over the notes of encouragement I read.

I received more love and encouragement that night from people I hardly knew than Jack had ever shown me in our entire married life. The warmth of Christian love and edification overwhelmed me and caused me to open my heart to hear what the Lord had to say.

The weekend retreat was the start of a new journey toward emotional and spiritual freedom, and it changed my views both on how I saw God and how Jack should treat me.

Teachable Moment

Some time after the retreat, Elizabeth gently confronted me about my inability to relax and have fun with friends. She told me that it would be emotionally healthy for me to have lunch with the ladies once in a while. She said it would renew my strength and revitalize my purpose as a wife, homeschool mom, and foster mom.

As Elizabeth coached me on how to be emotionally healthy, I began to realize how strict and controlling Jack was. He often made it impossible for me to do anything fun without making me feel guilty.

I watched how Rod treated Elizabeth with love, patience, and respect. My spirit soared with the hope that Jack would catch on to the relationship cues that had been modeled for us. Unfortunately, disappointment grew in my heart as Jack continued to weigh me down with words of condemnation and a spirit of control. But slowly, I was starting to see how his actions had affected just about every area of my life. Upon hearing Elizabeth's encouragement to invest my time into solid friendships, I began to examine the ways that I had been blocked from doing so over the course of my marriage.

The low self-esteem I developed over the years created many insecurities that interfered with my ability to form solid relationships with other women. I feared they would label me worthless and stupid, because that is how Jack made me feel and that is what I believed.

The other factor I had to remember was how Jack treated many of my friends when I would leave the room. He also criticized them after they left. I had found that it was easier to avoid my friends rather than listen to my husband pick apart their character.

Jack was very selective of my circle of friends, especially when it came to women who were independent thinkers. He wouldn't allow them to influence me with their self-reliant ideas and would ramble on about how they weren't positive role models for me.

With so much to consider, I realized an afternoon with the ladies would exert more energy than I had in reserve. I knew I needed to preserve my strength for Jack's behavioral swings and be available to protect the kids, in case he decided to unleash his unpredictable angry spirit.

I struggled to follow through with Elizabeth's ideas but tried anyway when my father invited me to a father-daughter banquet.

I was nervous about the kids being home alone with Jack for a long period of time without an accountability partner, like he'd had when I attended the ladies' retreat. I drove forty-five minutes south and planned to spend two days with my parents. Jack had had the opportunity to do that many times with his parents in years past, but this time it was my turn.

I glowed at the opportunity to grow closer to my family and it felt good to have them to myself. I was happy and decided to give a small speech at the banquet about how thankful I was that my dad loved me enough to adopt me. The event went so well that I planned to set more time aside for each parent in the months to follow.

After the banquet, Dad and I went back to the house to rest for a little bit. I lay on the couch with my eyes closed, until I heard the phone ring. I listened to my mother's voice fill with disappointment as she responded to the caller. "Ok, I'll let her know."

I released a deep sigh of frustration and rolled my eyes. I knew that the caller had been Jack. I waited for my mom to relay the message.

"Shelly, that was Jack. He's depressed and said that you need to come home because he can't handle you being away any longer."

My face grew hot with anger. My weekend plans had been hindered by a co-dependent control freak husband who only allowed me to have surface relationships with friends and family.

I heatedly packed my bags and threw everything in the car.

"I'm so sick of Jack dominating every area of my life!" I blurted out.

The drive home gave me time to cool off and think about how my relationship with him needed to change in order for the kids and me to thrive in a healthy environment.

I walked in the front door of my house and was briefly

greeted by the kids, but Jack was nowhere in sight. I went upstairs to our bedroom and found him engaged in video games on his computer. His whimsical expression quickly changed and he put on a look of despair when he became aware of my presence.

"Shelly, I don't do well when you are away that long. I need you here."

My jaw dropped open. *Unbelievable!* I thought. *I allowed him to do things with his family and friends but he dares not to extend the same courtesy to me?*

Elizabeth's suggestion to get away and refresh my spirit caused conflict for Jack and it exposed a weakness in him that confirmed my previous fears and speculations.

A few weeks later, Elizabeth's husband Rod talked to Jack about the way he treated the kids and me. When Jack walked into the house a couple of hours after leaving for his meeting with Rod, he slammed the front door behind him.

The kids had only just quietly scurried to their rooms to escape any ripple effect of their father's wrath when Jack stalked into the kitchen and began to scream at me. I couldn't understand him through his fury until he stated, "I will never go back to that church again! Nobody, and I mean *nobody*, has the right to tell me how to live my life. This is *my* family and I will treat you how I see fit!"

I was in shock and wondered how Jack thought it was okay to make a life decision to leave the church without my consent. We had many connections with our church family and we were faithfully involved in the homeschool group. The kids had been gaining much knowledge and many skills with sign language, drama, and other activities that were hard to accomplish without a group of students. I was upset that they would be cheated out of their weekly school activities and would be expected to leave their friends behind.

"We have been at that church for almost three years!" I pleaded with Jack. "Those people are family. Why do you want to rip us away from them?"

Jack stomped his feet on his way upstairs. "I will not talk about this with you anymore!" he called back in my direction. "My mind is made up!"

My heart broke for my children. They never had the stability they needed. Every town we moved to, every church we joined, and every friend they made had always been a temporary solution to fill an empty hole.

Jack needed to learn how to work through an offense and not run from everything he was upset about. I was seeing more clearly that life would always be the same everywhere we lived, until the day he could learn to be humble and reasonable.

I knew that it would be best if I was the one to tell the kids the bad news. Hesitantly, I started with Samantha, with the hope that I would gain enough courage to face the two older boys.

Samantha was initially sad and lost her smile for a few days, but later accepted the news without a hint of grief. I knew the kids were familiar with Jack's flighty decisions, but it disturbed me that she accepted the major change so quickly and easily. It made me wonder if she had learned to protect her heart by not getting too close to the friends she made.

Josiah was crushed that he would be cut off from his friends. He understood that he had no choice in Jack's decision, but wished for me to persuade Jack to rethink his choice to leave the church.

I sat down next to Peter on the couch, then gripped my hands together to contain my anxious spirit. I shared the news and watched him cry from the depths of his heart.

After I finished my last sentence, Peter tried to speak as he took in a deep breath. He raised his chest into the air and tilted his head back as if the wind had been knocked out of him. He held his breath a little longer than I expected, then let out a deep gasp of emotional pain. Finally he let out, "I feel like I'm all alone on an island with no friends."

I felt helpless and cried with him. I wanted to take his emotional pain and bear it all, just as I had done in years past.

I felt that the kids didn't deserve to deal with the consequences of Jack's rivalry with the church members and I could feel a spiteful spirit well up inside of me as I watched my son weep.

I didn't want to heed Jack's unreasonable rules of control for his own version of his personal utopia. Most of all, I wanted the freedom to speak the truth to my children about Jack's selfishness rather than defend it.

In years past, I had always trailed behind Jack to apologize to those he hurt along the way with his aggressive and offensive nature. He'd burned many bridges over the years and heartlessly left emotional scars on our family and friends. I was distraught because this time he was tearing at the hearts of our children and it was more than I could bear.

The kids lay down for a nap after our church talk. I sought comfort with a warm blanket and snuggled up on the couch. I thought about the consequences of Jack's selfish response and couldn't decide if I would dishonor my husband's decision to stay away from our church or if I would succumb to his wishes by being the submissive, docile wife he trained me to be. I bowed my head and asked the Lord for direction, but all I heard was silence.

Sparks of Discernment

Zoning

Imagine for a moment what a bull's-eye looks like. The bull's-eye that firefighters use contains three circles. The very center is called the hot zone. The hot zone is where assigned firefighters work to free victims from danger, for example, from a car crash. A couple of hot zone rules are to keep it clear from any tools not being used, and don't stand in it unless you have been assigned to work in that zone.

The zone outside the hot zone (the middle circle) is the warm zone. This is where assigned firefighters are to stand, ready to assist on command or take over the tasks of tired firefighters. Any unneeded firefighters or tools placed in the wrong zone will cause interference and possible injury.

The outside zone, the largest zone, is the cold zone. The cold zone is where all the excavation tools are kept so that they are in reach for the warm zone firefighters to grab and hand to those who are working in the hot zone.

When victims of abuse need assistance from an outside source, it is best to keep them safe in the cold zone or cleared from the scene. The only people that should be in the hot zone are those who work directly with the abuser to cool him or her off from their own abusive behaviors.

When family members choose to remain in the hot zone, they enable the abuser and further damage may occur. Therefore, it's best if all victims stay in the cool zone for a few days-- or even years, if need be-- until the all-clear command has been given from a counselor, pastors, and/or accountability partners.

"And this is the boldness we have in God's presence: that if we ask God for anything that agrees with what He wants, He hears us." (1 John 5:14).

No matter where you are in your journey, or in what zone you may find yourself, it is important to remember that there is help, and God does hear your pleas.

THIRTEEN

FUNNEL CLOUD OF TROUBLE

I struggled with sadness over Jack's decision to leave the church but when he expressed his desire to move back to Texas, I lost my sense of direction. My world grew dark and my thoughts spiraled down into a negative pit of hopelessness. The kids and I had been free from the bad memories of our Texas life and I feared that Jack would return to his old sinful habits if we moved back.

Peter, Josiah, and Samantha had grown to love the deep woods of Michigan and all the wildlife it contained. They wished to hunt and fish endlessly, and I knew those dreams would end for them if we moved back to Amarillo.

Jack's emotions had always been stable when we had foster

kids in the home. It was the only thing that broke his cycle of emotional maltreatment. He selflessly focused on the needs of the foster kids and was able to be a loving father figure to them. The foster kids loved the attention and interaction he gave them, and it seemed he was able to connect and understand them better than I did. He was also compassionate and creative when they needed to be redirected toward more appropriate behavior.

We no longer had foster kids in our home and I felt it would be best if we left it that way, until we were a healthy family again.

As my hardship increased, I searched for a self-help book that would not appear as a threat to Jack and would honor his wishes to keep our family issues private. I found a book written by Stormie Omartian, *The Power of A Praying Wife*. I knew Jack would approve of the title and he would think that I bought it to serve him better. My intentions with it were to help me keep my sanity from his indecisive and inconsiderate nature.

I read through the book to evaluate what I might be doing wrong to cause Jack's chaotic behavior. I also looked for the reason why he withheld his love and affection from me. I couldn't find an answer and in my time of crisis I cried out, "Why God, have You turned the heat up on the trials of my marriage? I don't know what to do."

I watched as Jack became more and more emotionally distant from the kids and me. He ignored us every night after work and chose not to speak during dinner time. He no longer participated in family readings, bonfires, or games. Instead, he turned his affections toward the computer. Jack successfully shut us out and acted as if we no longer existed. When he decided to talk, he growled with anger and commanded us around like an unhinged drill sergeant.

In spite of my sorrow, I kept Stormie's prayer book open for easy access. Her book gave me solace from Jack's mean-spirited ways and helped me keep my focus on the Lord. For three months I constantly prayed with the belief that the Lord would deliver the kids and me from Jack's ungodly behavior. But instead the trials continued to increase. One afternoon I became so distraught, I ran upstairs to our bedroom and looked out over the top of the pine trees. I gazed up to the heavens and asked God, "Why do You not hear my prayers? My life with my husband has worsened."

Tornado

Jack tried to rein in his unrighteous ways when he received an offer to take the position of youth and music pastor at a local church. As each day passed, he matured and it led me to believe that he had found his dream job. He enjoyed the people and led the music service with passion. The idea of moving to Texas got moved to the back burner.

Peter and Josiah learned to manage the soundboard at the church. I started a ladies' Bible study group and helped Jack with the youth group, until the day he emotionally shut down.

Jack went into a catatonic state on several different occasions and missed an unusual amount of work. He suddenly had no energy and could only sleep. I woke him for meals, but he would not eat. I encouraged him to see a doctor, but he refused medical treatment.

One day after work, he asked the boys to help him tie the muffler back up under the van. Excited, the boys ran out to the garage and waited for their father. A few minutes later, I heard

Jack yell and thought that one of the boys had dropped the tool box. I opened the front door of the house to listen but instead I met Josiah on the sidewalk.

"Mom, Dad threw tools at Peter and me, and he won't quit cursing at us."

"Did he hit you or Peter?" I asked with concern. "Are either of you hurt?"

Josiah shook his head no to both questions.

I walked out to the garage with Josiah and surprised Jack with my presence.

"What's going on out here?" I asked.

Jack answered with no shame, "Nothing, I'm good."

I took charge and told Jack that I needed the boys to help me in the kitchen.

After I listened to what the boys had to say about the garage incident, I thought it would be best to keep them close to me and away from Jack's unpredictable behavior.

I knew our family was in a spiritual battle, so I bowed my head and asked the Lord for wisdom. He laid on my heart to have each family member write a letter to Jack. We each wrote a note of praise and encouragement and explained how much we loved him. Each of us ended our note with how much we missed his fun personality and explained how we wished he would go see a doctor.

Jack read the letters and became irate. He left the house in a tizzy and slammed the door so hard that the front of the house shook. I worried that he may have misinterpreted the letters.

In my mind, Jack had no reason to be angry. First of all, he should have been happy that I didn't call the cops and have him detained. Secondly, I had every right to defend my children and provide a place of safety for them. Last of all, Jack was fortunate that I gave him a peaceful alternative to redeem his relationship with his children.

I wasn't sure where Jack drove off to in his moment of rage, or if he planned to return. My stomach turned sick when I checked the clock and realized that he had been gone for three hours. As time passed, I became concerned that we might get hit with an emotional tornado.

Everybody gathered together and stood still as Jack pulled up in the driveway. I tried to predict his mood before he walked inside but failed. At first he appeared calm as he pulled everyone together in the living room for a discussion. He seemed methodical in his attempt to respectfully and calmly hash out how the letters made him feel.

I tried to watch Jack's emotional cloud with caution, attempting to read his mood forecast as I'd become so accustomed to doing over the years. The emotional atmosphere started out with an eerie yellow tone, just as the sky does to warn of the possibility of a tornado. But suddenly it turned to a sickly green color, just as the sky does to warn that the tornado's arrival is imminent. The storm started to rev up with an unpredictable wind when Jack's demeanor suddenly changed.

"Since all of you are unappreciative for the things I have provided for you over the years and can't seem to understand how hard I work every day, I have spent one hundred dollars to reward myself for all that I've contributed to this family," he said.

Jack threw a bag on the floor and pulled out his first purchase to flaunt it. The tension in his face grew and his voice spewed a level of bitterness as he continued to show off his finds. There was nothing particularly special about his purchases-- some clothing, entertainment, some odds and ends-- but he was bound and determined to show us that he was entitled to whatever he desired or thought was necessary for himself, regardless of our opinions.

We all sat in silence and uneasiness while we waited for Jack to lose his temper. We could sense it coming, but we weren't prepared for the magnitude of the wrath aimed in our direction. The uncensored language that flew out of Jack's filthy mouth grated in my ears. At that moment I knew he had snapped. He had held back the majority of his sinful behaviors and lifestyle for nine years, since the time he was saved in Texas. Now he unleashed it all at once. I sat in shock as he attacked the character of each family member with inappropriate, raw verbiage.

"Jack, you have no right to talk to us that way."

Jack turned in my direction and pointed his angry finger at me. The same finger he used on the day he threw the highchair through the living room wall and shouted that he would hunt me down and kill me if I ever left him.

"You shut up and stay out of this," Jack's voice thundered. "These are my children and I will do what I want!"

I remembered this angry person from the first six years of our marriage and knew he had officially returned. I heard my inner voice speak, *Grab the kids and go.* I was scared of Jack and what he might do if the kids and I walked past him. I was scared I would exacerbate the situation and put them in the path of physical harm. Instead, Jack stood up and left the room, and the heat of his anger followed him.

The kids sat in shock with their eyes glazed over, while I struggled to clean up the aftermath of the emotional tornado.

Jack had never spoken to us that way before. I was speechless. The ears of our children had been violated with words of hate that devalued and demeaned them. I could not undo or restore their confidence in a week's time. My prayers lifted to heaven, "Why, Lord, have You allowed this to happen? I don't understand."

I had just witnessed the worst damage in our history from Jack's abusive speech. I couldn't believe that the same man who rescued Josiah off the side of a cliff had just destroyed the self-confidence, self-worth, and dignity of our children in the matter of fifteen minutes. Jack had officially taken his tyrannical behavior to a whole new level by now including the children in the browbeating sessions he usually reserved for me.

There were many times that Jack had confessed his desire to break the legacy of abuse in his family lineage. I wasn't sure if physical abuse had ever taken place in our home but I was positive that his verbal assaults caused just as much damage as physical abuse, since it was neither appropriate nor healthy.

Spiritual Awareness

The Holy Ghost was more active in my life since my co-workers had prayed over me, two years before the emotional tornado happened. I began to see our problems from a spiritual perspective, exploring solutions to negate his actions.

After the emotional storm blew over, the kids and I quietly tiptoed around the house for a few days to avoid another angry outburst. I didn't feel that I should apologize to him for how he mistreated us. Instead, for the first time ever, I waited for him to apologize to us.

Jack expressed to me that he was offended and felt we

persecuted him when we wrote the letters. Because of this, the tension from the silent treatment hung in the air longer than I expected.

In the past, Jack would turn the events around to blame me for his actions. But this time I saw it differently. I knew that neither the kids nor I deserved the ungodly behavior and disrespect he poured on us.

After three days of silence, I grew anxious because Jack hadn't apologized to us yet. I couldn't take the tension any longer. It seemed as if it hung over the house like a stretched-out rubber band, ready to snap any minute. I didn't want another tornado to let loose. Though I knew that I was not at fault for the emotional devastation, and neither were the kids, I felt I needed to protect us from Jack's cruelty, and history had taught me that that often meant catering to his twisted will. I walked upstairs and apologized. I acted as if I were regretful, but in my heart I knew full well it was Jack who should apologize. "Jack, I'm sorry."

Jack responded as if he'd had every right to act the way he did. His voice grew somber as he spoke in deep, serious tones. He stayed focused on the computer screen, clicking on his picks for his football leagues. He never bothered to look up at me when he spoke.

"You know I love you don't you?"

I usually wept after Jack broke the silence with his first sentence. I didn't understand it but for whatever reason, this time I couldn't cry. I remained quiet to see if Jack had any remorse for the way he acted. I listened as his words turned warm but noticed that his emotional connection with me remained cold. He continued, "I would never marry again if I couldn't have you."

I was stunned as I listened with my spiritual ears. I was aware that that statement couldn't possibly be true, given the number of affairs he'd had in the past. I digested the words he spoke but felt like throwing up as he continued.

"There is no other woman who could understand me like you do and I mean that. I will never leave you."

I was fully aware that I was in a twisted situation, and recognized that he had used the same phrases to reassure me in previous blowups. I began to connect his body language, somber behavior, and the words he spoke as part of his dramatic presentation at the end of each explosive behavior cycle he'd had in the past. I now realized that it was his attempt to make me feel guilty, unworthy, and as if the situation was all my fault.

With each behavior cycle, Jack would first unleash his anger on me. Then for three days after that, he would go to great lengths to win my affection through words of reassurance. This time, I was not assured. I saw the deception that existed in our relationship through the mind games he played.

I was unsure if Jack's behavior issues were because of a fake salvation experience or if he was acting out because of his unresolved childhood issues.

The longer I thought about the situation, the more in tune I became with the lack of desire he had to demonstrate the fruits of the Spirit that the Bible talks about in **Galatians 5:22-23**. These are characteristics that manifest themselves over a period of time during a Christian's life, such as love, joy, peace, patience, kindness, goodness, faithfulness, gentleness, and self-control. He might pass off one or two of these characteristics at a time and maybe even all of them during a small group meeting, but now I wondered if it was all a farce. My eyes were being opened to the concept that Jack chose to display those benevolent characteristics only to impress or trick others, distracting them from who he really was.

Jack's behavior was so irrational that I wondered if he was on recreational drugs. I searched his belongings and checked all the pockets in his wardrobe and other possible areas he might hide them. I never found anything. He didn't drink alcohol nor did he smoke. His cold and calculated behavior was unexplained and it left me puzzled.

I had tried to show compassion and grace toward Jack over the years but now I felt burdened as I carried around his baggage full of bricks named sorrow, regret, and worthlessness.

As Jack's wife and Biblical helper, I had believed that it was my job to heal his hurts, uplift his ego, and build his self-confidence. But I suddenly realized that I no longer had the stamina, skills, or resources needed to fix my husband.

Blood Brothers

Because of Jack's mean spirit, I called his parents to reach out for help. Jack shared his struggles with them and agreed to see a doctor. His life began to level out. However, there was no spark in his eyes and it caused him to be emotionally despondent from time to time. In spite of that, he was well enough to return to work, after another period of absence due to his mental health issues.

Six weeks after medical care, Jack decided to do some yard work. The kids happened to follow him outside to play. I stayed in the house to clean up the kitchen after our large breakfast of pancakes, scrambled eggs, and sausages. Suddenly I noticed that it seemed oddly quiet outside. I wandered to the back door of the house and opened it.

"Jack, what are you doing?" I called.

Surprised, Jack's wide eyes revealed that he'd been caught. "I made a gash on Peter's hand and my hand," he said. "We are blood brothers now. I told Peter about the bond that blood brothers have and explained to him that we would never leave each other."

His words caught me off guard and my face turned to stone. I couldn't believe what I was hearing.

After a long pause I asked as calmly as possible, "Do you really think that was necessary and appropriate for a parent to do with a thirteen-year-old son?"

Jack looked at me and said, "Come on, we all did this when we were in school. I'd rather have him do this with me than with a kid who has some bloodborne disease."

I couldn't connect with Jack's logic but tried to make sense of it. "Peter has never heard of blood brothers. What made you think you needed to do this?"

Jack stood up and let go of Peter's hand. "Since he doesn't have any friends, I wanted him to know that he could always count on me."

I walked over to Peter and looked down at his hand. "Really, Jack? We pricked our fingers with a pin when we were in school."

"It's not that bad," Jack insisted. He held the palm of his hand up. "Look at my hand, it's the same size cut on Peter's hand. I placed the cut in the crease so we would feel the pain each time we use our hands, to reinforce the pact we made with each other on this day."

I doctored up Peter's hand and looked him in the eye. "Did

you want to do this?"

"Yes I did," he gave me his words of assurance.

I waited for Peter to say more, but he spoke as if Jack had never convinced him to do such a thing. I took in a deep sigh and let Peter go, then walked up to Jack, stared him in the eyes and spoke with a firm voice.

"Never, ever do anything like this again with any of our children!" I snapped.

I ran upstairs to get away from Jack's insanity and to mentally hash out what Jack had done. *What is abuse? Abuse is when a parent beats their child, often leaving black and blue marks. Am I right about this? I have never heard of a parent doing anything like what Jack just did with Peter.*

I disapproved of Jack's blood brother idea. I asked myself again if this constituted physical abuse. I couldn't say yes, because it wasn't a bruise, but I couldn't say no because it was just too bizarre to accept.

I sat on my bed to think through the incident. *Why did Jack need to be blood brothers with his biological son, born with his DNA? Maybe Jack plans to divorce me and wants to use the blood brother pact to manipulate Peter into believing that he must choose his dad over me.*

Sparks of Discernment

Finding Help

"Get all the advice you can, and you will succeed; without it you will fail." (**Proverbs 15:22 GNT**).

You might be surprised to find just how many stories are similar to mine. King Solomon put it this way, "There is nothing new under the sun." (**Ecclesiastes 1:9b NIV**).

However, the important thing to remember is to seek help outside of your family unit. The burden is too heavy for one person to carry alone and you need an outside perspective for your particular situation.

Lavender

Three months after Jack's emotional tornado blew over, the pastor's wife from the church we'd left brought me a little clay pot filled with artificial lavender flowers. Her visit encouraged me, given the intense trials I'd recently endured. She handed me the flowers then said, "The Lord wanted me to bring this to you and tell you that you are supposed to move to Texas."

Jack had mentioned moving to Texas, but no plans had yet been set in stone. My messenger left and I took her words in with reverence as if the Lord had spoken them Himself. I placed the tiny flowers by the kitchen sink to remind me of the move that would soon happen and that it was what God wanted us to do.

God knew how to get my attention, for lavender had recently become my favorite flower. The kids and I had found some on one of our walks through town. We would often stand by the beautiful plant to take in the smell on our walks to the fire station to see what rescue projects the firefighters had trained for.

Comforted

In March of 2005, Jack made the plans to move our family to Texas in May.

I cried. I felt as if my world had caved in, in spite of what my lavender-messenger had shared with me. On the one hand, I knew that a move back to Texas near Stella and Wayne might fulfill Jack's desire to have a solid relationship with his parents and possibly lead to a healthier environment for the kids. But I also remembered that every time we moved away from my parents, Jack became promiscuous.

I fell into a pit of despair as I thought about a new start away from our beautiful green trees and the smells of fresh water and pine. I didn't want to leave my siblings and parents again, for I knew a long distance move would make it tough to stay in touch.

My sorrow deepened, until one night it was as if the Holy Ghost washed away all my worries and anxiety. He gave me a verse to cling to:

> "But I tell you the truth, it is better for you that I go away. When I go away, I will send the Helper to you. If I do not go away the Helper will not come." **(John 16:7)**.

I knew that I was not alone and that I had the ability to live a peaceful life because the Holy Spirit was in me. I didn't have to call on Him, I just needed to listen and allow Him to work through me and trust Him with our move to Texas.

Sparks of Discernment

Empty Oxygen Tank

A firefighter's oxygen tank provides him or her with clean air when chemicals and carbon dioxide are a danger to their well-being. Each tank provides anywhere between 30 to 60 minutes of oxygen, depending on how much their air cylinder can hold. When the firefighter is working hard or becomes anxious, he or she will use their oxygen faster, and must leave the hot zone sooner.

Victims should evaluate how full their oxygen tank is, and also check the kids' tanks.

Oxygen, in this case, refers to the mental state of each individual. Refilling your cylinder would entail participating in joyful and healthy activities.

When the abuse is intense, it's best to find someplace else to stay. I realize some may choose not to leave, and there could indeed be hope that your situation could be remedied. However, I am by no means encouraging you to stay in an abusive situation. I strongly advise against it for your own safety.

Take a moment to assess your oxygen tank levels, or your mental health, by considering things like depression, appetite, bad dreams, and physical discomfort like headaches, stomachaches, and shortness of breath. Chart your answers for each family member and email the result to your doctor, so that there is a record to prove that you and your kids were under duress, if you end up needing to show evidence in a court of law. For a more detailed evaluation, look at the **Activities and Resources For Recovery** in the back of the book.

It's not uncommon for abuse victims to suffer from some or all of the types of symptoms listed above and more, and there's no shame in getting help when you need it. Thankfully, there are a lot of things your doctor can do for you to help keep you safe.

If the oxygen in a firefighter's tank is reading that it's in the red, then that firefighter has 15 minutes left before he or she is on empty. In the same way, being in the red with your mental and emotional health will leave you physically weak, mentally vulnerable, and susceptible for more victimization from your abuser. The abuser will see it as an opportunity to intensify the abuse, until you are pushed into a state of depression.

"You make known to me the path of life." (Psalm 16:11a NIV)

There *is* a path out of your darkness.

FOURTEEN

911, WHAT'S YOUR EMERGENCY?

*A*t the end of May, after the snow lifted, we set off for Texas. When we arrived, I noticed that Amarillo hadn't seemed to change at all from eight years prior.

We took the Washington Street exit and made our way a few blocks over to where Stella and Wayne lived.

Jack opened the back of the moving truck and began to unload our treasures. I paused for a moment and allowed my gaze to lock onto the fire station through the trees north of us. I felt an indescribable peace as I watched the American flag flying freely in the warmth of the Texas sun. I took in a deep breath and looked up at the blue Amarillo sky, feeling the eyes of the Lord look down at me. I felt safe and knew we had made the right decision.

I looked over to see a tall, bald man walking out from the backyard with a set of hedge trimmers in his hand. He approached my in-laws with a confident, serious air about him as he collected his check for the yard work he'd completed. As he went on his way, Stella turned to us and gushed about what a great gardener he was. Apparently he was the only groundskeeper who had ever met her expectations as a worthy caretaker. On top of his reputable groundskeeping skills, he was also working on becoming a full-time firefighter. As Wayne and Stella continued to sing his praises, I began to develop an idea of the man's character. He seemed to encompass the respectable and admirable qualities of a hard-working individual who was striving to make a positive difference in the world. Something stuck in the back of my mind then, and it wasn't until years later that I would realize that it was a small glowing ember that would grow into a flame of desire to pursue work in firefighting myself.

Josiah's interest in firefighting also grew and I was excited to hear that the Amarillo Fire Department offered a Junior Cadet Program. I hoped to sign him up after we were settled in our new home.

We lived with Stella and Wayne throughout the summer of 2005, then began to discuss the prospect of purchasing their house from them. In the midst of this dynamic life change, Jack stopped his depression medication each time he began to feel better. His cycle of depression became a constant, and it brought chaos to our lives.

There were many days I poured all my energy into Jack. He struggled with the purpose to live and searched for his self-worth as a husband and father.

In the months to follow, Jack confessed his desire to give up on life and become a hobo. He encouraged me to pack the kids up and move back to Michigan. I would attempt to redirect his thoughts with a positive light, but his views created a black hole that tried to suck me into the same depressive state he was in.

Jack's depressive episodes lasted for weeks and within that time, I encountered many unwelcome spiritual influences. I did my best to pray and read scriptures to combat the forces in that spiritual war. After the first few weeks of this ongoing cycle, I grew weary of the battle and reached out to Stella and Wayne for spiritual direction.

Wayne took charge and led our family in a prayer meeting a few different times. Jack's depression would dissipate, but return with intensity weeks later.

In the meantime, Stella created discord and began to speak in slanderous ways about me. After being married to Jack for fifteen years, I now knew where he had picked up his insidious behavior of maltreatment.

I quietly watched from the corner of my eye as she took her victims aside and belittled their character for multiple hours. The most evident case was Wayne. Jack had also confided in me at one point that there were many times that he had been on the receiving end of her criticisms as well. I had no doubt, based on what I witnessed, that she regularly sought out ways to put others down. The result of her demeaning diatribe would leave her victim with a broken spirit and low self-esteem. There would be no tears, for it was the individual's spirit that mourned deep within his or her soul. The only evidence left for others to observe would be a lack of joy and a somber demeanor. Three days would pass, before he or she would begin to smile again and express the freedom they felt inside. When Stella noticed that the carefree spirit of her prey had returned, she would bully them back into a downtrodden disposition.

I recognized this behavior all too well. Jack was known to do the same thing to me on a regular basis. It was then that I realized that the chain of physical abuse had been broken, but the emotional abuse still remained.

The Canyon

The kids and I felt the strain of tight living quarters while we lived with Stella and Wayne. To lighten the stress, we made plans to take a day trip to Palo Duro Canyon in Canyon, Texas. We longed for the great outdoors and could hardly wait to take in the fresh air and sunshine.

I held my breath and gripped the arms of the seat as we drove in first gear down the steep curvy road into the canyon. I was intimidated by the large boulders on the hillside and noticed that they were big enough for our whole family to fit into, had they been hollow. I kept an eye on them to be sure none broke loose. The boulders had been known to roll over hikers without a moment's notice.

We were warned about the dangers of rattlesnakes, scorpions, and flash floods in the canyon, but we never imagined that we would be directly involved with a 911 emergency that day.

We started out by hiking a trail that we had never seen before. The deep orange colors of the trail led us up a path along some large, dusty mammoth rocks. The scenery was awe-inspiring, but the drop-off below was treacherous. The kids began to run and jump from one rock to the next. I caught my breath in horror as

I watched their shoes slip over the pebbles beneath their feet.

"Get back on the trail and don't run!" I yelled.

For the first time ever in relation to parenting, Jack undermined my authority and casually yelled back, "Stay where you are, you're fine. Nothing bad will happen to you."

I pleaded my case before Jack, reminding him of the cliff Josiah slid down the last time we lived out west. He didn't seem too bothered. I turned around and yelled back at him, "Don't you care anymore? What has happened to you?"

Jack turned away from me and quickened his pace to put a greater distance between us. Later, we met up at the car to look for another trail. We happened to stumble upon the same old washed-out cave that we had visited ten years ago.

"Let's go up there and see if our names are still carved into the side of the cave wall!" Jack yelled out with excitement.

The hike was a familiar attraction for many youth groups and summer camps, and we figured that the rough terrain didn't possess any real danger.

We hiked up the steep trail of large stones to the bend in the path and let the kids take a breather. The journey was no easy task! Jack decided to share with me that he had canceled our life insurance policy and closed out all of our savings accounts.

"Why did you do that?" I confronted him immediately. "You promised me that we would keep those things in place."

"We'll be fine," Jack replied with a smirk. "You just have to trust me."

I turned away from him to get control of my anger and noticed that we had left the view of the paved road below. After a few minutes I yelled out, "Let's go, the kids are bored."

On the hike up to the cave, I went into prayer. "Lord, I'm

miserable! My life with Jack has worsened. He is so cruel and acts as if he doesn't want the responsibility of a family. I can't live like this anymore. I feel as if I am falling apart from the inside out because of the constant stress I am under."

I pleaded with the Lord as the tears began to roll down my face. "Lord, I want a divorce."

I finished my prayer just as we approached the mouth of the cave. Then something unbelievable happened right before my eyes.

Peter wanted to climb up onto a natural loft that was encased ten feet up inside the cave. He looked to the right side of the cave wall to test a row of embedded rocks and noticed that the middle rock was loose. He pulled it out. We all stood silent with doubt in our eyes, as Peter inquisitively held the rock that was shaped like a football.

A few moments passed before Peter broke the silence. "I don't think it's safe to climb up the row of rocks on the cave wall." He turned to Jack. "Dad, will you hoist me up to the loft?"

Peter safely made it up with Jack's help, then quickly paced the little area that had been carved out by the rain. Josiah stood just inside the cave, looking up at his brother, while Samantha and I stood outside the mouth of the cave.

Samantha and I screamed, and I couldn't get the words out fast enough. "Jack, look out!"

Peter and Josiah joined in, "Dad, move out of the way!"

The cave wall that once held the football-shaped stone, where Peter had considered climbing first, cracked in slow motion and began to release from the side of the cave. Jack looked back at us with confusion as he tried to process why we were shouting.

Just then, a thirteen-by-five-foot sandstone wall fell and split apart on the ledge that Jack was standing on. Large chunks of rock flew in every direction. Some hit Josiah, but the largest sections of the wall hit Jack. I looked down below as the rocks tumbled down the four-foot drop and onto the stone path that trailed back to the road. I went into a trance and experienced a moment of tunnel vision. I was so glad that Peter hadn't climbed up the side of the wall. All I could think about was how he would have been pummeled and buried beneath a pile of rubble.

I helped Peter off the cliff then turned to help Jack. He was down for the count. I anxiously ran to his aid as he struggled to sit up, and I quickly changed my prayer from before. "Lord, I am sorry, please forgive me for being selfish. I'll work through this marital conflict with Jack, just let him live. The kids need their father."

Jack fought to stay awake but his head bobbed and his neck eventually went limp. I looked over his thighs and noticed that the back of them were already covered with dark purple bruises from the impact of the fallen rocks. His right calf had been sliced open with a wound where a disturbing amount of blood oozed to create a quickly growing pool under his leg.

I wasn't sure how stable the cave was, and feared a delayed chain reaction. I knew Jack would prefer to be alive and paralyzed rather than dead underneath a layer of sandstone, so I made the decision to move him.

"Jack, wake up!" I yelled.

I placed my knuckles between his two collar bones then applied pressure to help him regain consciousness.

"Stop, that hurts!" Jack cried out.

"Sorry," I said. "But you have to stay awake and if that's what it takes, I'll do it again."

Peter and I faced each other on either side of Jack. We helped him sit up, then attempted to make a sort of seat for him with our arms. Lifting from under his thighs and supporting his back, we began to move. Jack screamed out again, "Ouch, ah, stop, it hurts!"

Peter and I stopped to set Jack down, then re-positioned our hands to a less tender area. We moved Jack down the trail until we were out of range from falling rocks.

When we finally made it to the bend in the trail, Peter and I set Jack on a large flat rock to rest. Jack struggled to stay awake while we waited for someone to drive by. I was unable to pick up a signal on my cell phone, and knew that God was the only one I could count on to bring help our way.

With hesitation, I sent Josiah and Samantha down the trail to wave down the next car. Their task was to ask a tourist to run and get help. For their own safety, I commanded them not to get in the car with anyone. In the meantime I continued my conversation with God, only out loud this time. "I can't be both places at once, Lord, please send us a family to run for help, and please keep Josiah and Samantha safe!"

Minutes passed before an elderly couple stopped to hear what Josiah and Samantha had to say. I watched as they pointed up the trail in Jack's direction. Once the older couple spotted us, they immediately left to report the accident to the DNR officer on duty.

It seemed like hours before the paramedics arrived. They made the hike look quite difficult as they walked up the trail with their heavy medical equipment.

One of the medics looked Jack over. He began to question if he should call for a helicopter lift when he noticed a trail of blood trickling down from Jack's right ear. I beckoned the medic to look at the wound on Jack's forehead, informing him that the blood trailed down instead from the head injury and into the ear. There seemed to be a collective sigh of relief upon the realization that Jack was not bleeding out of his ear, as that would have been an indication of serious head trauma.

While the medic secured Jack to a gurney, Jack masked his anger and irresponsibility by keeping the paramedics amused with his wit. They had not had to deal with Jack's mean, spiteful ways, and they were unaware of what he had recently put the kids and me through. To them, he was charming and fun.

I hoped that Jack would see the cave accident as a wake-up call from God. But instead, he viewed the accident as an act of love from the Lord because his life had been spared.

FIFTEEN

BLACK SMOKE BREWING

Our first summer in Texas came to an end and the sale of our house in Grawn, Michigan was final. We were going through with the purchase of Wayne and Stella's house, but Stella wasn't quite ready to let go of her cherished abode. What started out as a happy family reunion with Jack's parents ended on a sour note for Stella. She made me aware of her discontent toward selling us their house when she opened the door to our school room and began to yell, "This is my house! This is my house! This is my house!"

I remained calm and realized that she was trying to instigate a fight. Calmly, I bit my tongue. I then told her that she could keep her house and I wasn't going to fight her for it. She was unsure how she should respond to my comment, so she turned away and opted to give us the silent treatment.

As what seemed to be a last stand of defiance, three days before Stella and Wayne moved out, they camped out in the living room and let the air conditioner run continuously at 62 degrees Fahrenheit. The three days of refrigeration left us with a very large electric bill.

Jack seemed content when his parents moved out, and I was glad to have freedom over the kitchen again. Life went better for us in the weeks to follow as we focused our attention on remodeling projects and pushed aside our issues with Stella.

While Jack and I put wallpaper up in the master bathroom, he returned to his rude, demeaning ways.

"What are you doing?" I asked, squinting my eyes at him quizzically. "Why are you treating me this way?"

Jack looked up at me with a gleam in his eye. "See, I can be a jerk if I want to," he taunted, as if that explained anything.

I let out a deep sigh. "Why do you have so much venom toward me?"

Jack winked. "Don't worry, it's all okay."

Jack's cruel spirit ceased but I felt he used the wallpaper project to test how much mistreatment I would take.

The kids painted their rooms. We pulled up the old carpet in the living room and kitchen areas to expose the beautiful wood floors below. In the guest bathroom, we removed the old tiles from the wall and planned to put a shower in.

In the fall, we joined a homeschool group and made some new friends. Peter was voted in as president of the student council and became actively involved with community projects.

I realized that my firstborn son hit a mark of maturity when he shared his prayer time with me.

"Mom," he said. "God has called me to be a missionary to

Africa."

It was hard for me to hear, and I rejected the news. "Peter, there is a lot of work to be done in the United States," I said. "Maybe you should consider home missions."

"No mom, I know it's Africa," Peter answered with confidence.

I didn't want my son to go to Africa. I wanted to be the grandmother who had giggling grandchildren running around her house after a nice Sunday dinner.

I couldn't understand why God allowed Jack to be mean to me and why He wanted to send Peter away to Africa. I asked God, "What else do you want to take from me?" In the fog of my day-to-day struggles with Jack, it was getting harder to see and understand God's plans and blessings through the trials that seemed to branch into every aspect of my life.

In February of 2006, Jack tested me again. He asked the kids and me to meet him in the family room. Jack sat on the hearth of the fireplace to soak in its warmth, and after a few minutes he said, "I want to try something."

He studied our faces with a serene smile, then closed the flue to the chimney.

"Jack, what are you doing?" I yelled. "Open that back up."

Jack put his hands out in front of him to signal for us to be quiet.

"It's okay, I just want to try something," he calmly repeated.

Peter became apprehensive and stood up. With a stern voice, Jack commanded him to sit back down. Within three minutes, the room began to fill with toxic fumes.

"That's enough, open it back up now!" I yelled out.

Jack wouldn't give an explanation for why he'd closed the flue, and I wondered why he felt it necessary to test our trust level. After Jack's experiment, he emotionally separated himself from the rest of the family. For everyone's safety, I found a counselor and Jack agreed to go.

The counselor asked if Jack was on any psychiatric medication. Instantly, Jack became defensive and made it clear that he did not want to go that route. However, I didn't care what the counselor had to do to get Jack's emotions and bizarre behavior under control.

The counselor worked with Jack for six weeks then said, "That's all he needs. He's done. I've given him the tools he needs for recovery and now it's up to him to make the right choices."

Jack didn't lose control of his temper much after that but instead, he wept uncontrollably and suffered from anxiety attacks. I took him to work every day so he wouldn't be able to come home early. Often, after the first hour of his shift, he would call and beg me to pick him up. I always encouraged him to stay another hour, and told him to call me then if he didn't have his anxiety under control. When he finished the second hour of his shift, he would call again and beg me to pick him up for a second time. Somehow I always managed to talk him into working a third hour.

I picked up a job to help with the bills in spite of how Jack felt about me being in the workforce. I knew the kids would be okay since my job was only one block away.

I worked twenty hours a week as a receptionist at a busy hair salon. The job inspired me to pursue a career in cosmetology, but first I knew I would have to convince Jack that it would be profitable. Before I confronted him, I organized my thoughts and wrote down how I would manage to do the housework, go to school three days a week, and keep my job.

When I finally presented my idea, Jack lowered his eyes to the ground and then spoke with hesitation.

"I told you that if you ever worked outside the home, I would make your life absolute torture," he said. "But because we need the money, an education would bring us more income. I'll let you do it, if you can keep up with all your household obligations."

I felt like I had just been given a new set of wings. I was excited to go back to school in the fall of 2006. During that time, I managed to keep my part-time job as a receptionist with the expectation that I would work there as a stylist after graduation.

The first eight weeks went well, and Jack seemed to settle into the new routine with no fight. I managed to keep up with the housework and have a homemade dinner on the table, even after ten hours of school.

I lost weight, gained independence, and developed self-confidence. I was extremely happy that I had a social life at school that Jack couldn't control.

Toward the end of October, Jack's loyalties toward me began to shift. He badgered me about being at school on Saturdays. I always listened to his complaints.

"You never watch me play computer games anymore," he would say.

It was one of those things that I did to keep peace in our family. Jack didn't want my attention focused on a book or television screen, nor did he interact with me while he played the games. It was just something he expected me to do. I was always bored and thought it was a senseless thing, but for some reason he needed my visible support as he battled the tribes in his war games.

As my self-esteem grew, Jack begged me to gain weight. I was shocked. I liked my new look and the energy I had. He tried a new approach. He bought me a candy bar every day.

"Here, I brought this home for you. It's your reward for losing weight."

"Jack, I don't want the candy bar," I replied. "Give it to one of the kids."

"I buy you something nice and this is what I get?" he yelled. "Rejection?"

Jack then began to feel paranoid about where I was on the days I went shopping. He tracked my transactions through our online bank account and took notes of how long I was at each store, what I spent, and how long it took me to get from one destination to the next.

I became aware of Jack's new insecurities but never understood them, since I had never given him a reason to question me. I didn't like the way his overprotective talons tightened their grip, holding me down and invading my freedom.

Next, Jack begged me to quit my job at the salon. For weeks he badgered me over the issue. I didn't see how it would be a wise choice, since we were facing bankruptcy.

"No, Jack!" I spoke my mind. "We hardly have enough money to feed the kids. I am not going to quit my job."

I ignored Jack's wishes and he distanced himself from me.

Jack didn't bother to recognize my birthday that year, which was unusual for him. In the past, he'd always given me my gift a couple of weeks early. I knew that when he intentionally "forgot," our relationship was in serious jeopardy.

Sparks of Discernment

Identifying Toxicity

A firefighter is not only equipped to handle fire, but trained to identify what is burning and have knowledge of its toxicity level. Firefighters know which items, such as furniture, give off toxic chemicals and can cause immediate death when inhaled. It is important for firefighters to wear their self-contained breathing apparatus (mask and oxygen tank) to all calls involving smoke and fire.

You may be able to identify your spouse's toxic behavior, just as a firefighter can identify what toxins are being burned. Because of this, you may feel you are able to use your own self-contained breathing apparatus to initiate intervention for your abuser. But I want you to remember that you are the victim. Just as a fire will consume a civilian who is not equipped to handle the flame, you are not professionally trained to deal with the toxicity level of verbal, sexual, or physical assault committed against you and your family.

This also applies to those who have had someone confide in them about an abusive experience. The best thing that you can do for a loved one who has opened up to you about being abused is to offer your love and support, but to encourage them (or go with them) to talk to a doctor, counselor, or law enforcement official.

SIXTEEN

MULTI-VORTEX TORNADO OF BEHAVIORS

*I*n February of 2007, I became afraid of Jack's emotional imbalance. One evening after I arrived home from work, I looked for him at his computer desk. He wasn't there. I left the family room and yelled down the hall, "Jack, where are you?"

I checked all the rooms in the house, then looked outside. I still couldn't find him. I went back in the house and made my way to the bedroom. When I tried to open the closet door, the old door knob wouldn't budge. I tried again, but the handle still wouldn't move. I gave the door a hearty knock before I asked, "Jack, are you in there?"

There was no movement in the closet and I wasn't sure if he was in there or not. I tried the door knob again but I was unable to turn it in either direction.

I placed my ear against the door. Silence hummed in the air. I spoke louder, only this time with more authority.

"Jack, if you're in there, I need you to open the door."

There was no sound. I stood by the closet door for a few more minutes before walking away, but then I recalled a similar incident in the past. He did this same exact thing when Peter was three years old. He held the door handle so tight that I couldn't get it to wobble. I walked away for a few minutes, then came back and tried again and it opened. *Maybe if I walk away from the door, he'll do the same thing again.*

I tiptoed to the door then quickly grabbed the door handle with the hope that I would outsmart him. I failed. I quietly stepped back and waited, but impatience turned to anger. Finally, I charged the door.

"I don't have time for this stupidity!" I shouted louder and tried to shake the door. "Jack, I know you're in there, open it, open the door now!"

I relentlessly knocked on the door, louder and louder. There was still no answer.

I groaned out of frustration, then walked back out to the hallway and hid around the corner to see what would happen. As I stood still, I began to think about Jack's battle with depression. *The clothes in the closet hang on a heavy steel rod that is securely in place.* My eyes grew big. *Jack keeps his belts in there.* I gasped. *What if Jack has hung himself?*

I ran back to the closet door, this time with urgency. "Jack, open the door! Open it now or I will call the police!"

At last, he responded. "Leave me alone," he said. "I want to be left alone in here. Don't call the police."

"You don't have that choice, Jack," I answered. "You must open the door or I will call the police."

"Alright!" Jack responded in fear, then opened the door. "Just don't call the police, you know how much I hate them!"

The next day I gave my two weeks' notice at the salon so I could monitor Jack's behavior while he was home with the kids. On the days I went to school, I told them to call me if their dad happened to make it home before I did.

One Saturday afternoon I arrived home shortly after Jack. I looked all over the house for him. This time I found him unresponsive while he sat on the commode. He sat there staring off into space as if nobody else existed.

"Jack, what's wrong?" I asked.

Jack remained still until he decided to talk. He spoke without emotion in a monotone voice.

"It wouldn't take much to walk over the line," he said. "It's just one step over the line."

"What do you mean, Jack?"

"Everyone has it in them to take a step over the line to kill somebody."

I shuddered and swallowed my fear.

"Jack, who is it that you want to kill?" I asked.

Jack responded, as if he were under a spell, "It doesn't matter who. I just have the need to kill somebody, anybody."

I became nervous in the weeks to follow as I watched Jack feed his twisted thoughts. He studied the personal testimonies of convicted killers, their premeditated thoughts, and the methods they used to kill their families. At the end of each biography, each murderer shared how they misled the authorities with false information, so they wouldn't become a suspect.

"Hey, Jack."

There was no response from him when I tried to break his concentration from the television.

"Jack, when do you want dinner?" I spoke more loudly.

He turned my way, then studied me as if I were to become his murder victim. A chill coursed through my body, followed by the weight of his homicidal vibe.

A few weeks later he watched a movie about a man who tried to kill his girlfriend, then shoved her body in a portable dumpster, locking her wounded body in a space he rented at a storage facility. Jack caught me off guard when he looked up at me then blurted out, "Huh, I never thought to put a body in there. That's a really good idea."

Would Jack really try to do that to me or is he just trying to scare me? I wondered. *The only reason he wanted to kill me in the past was because he was involved with another woman. Did Jack have another woman in his life now?*

I shook my head in disgust at this man who claimed to be a Christian, then huffed as I recalled Stella's advice about Jack's problem with lying.

"I want you to know that Jack was a compulsive liar when he was a child," she'd said. "I want to warn you that his ears turn red when he is lying about something."

Whenever I asked Jack if he was involved with another woman, he would stand tall and command my attention with his nonverbal cues, locking eyes with me. He would intimidate me with a creepy stare, never allowing my gaze to leave his. Because of this behavior, I never remembered to check his ears to see if they were red.

I remained neutral and showed no fear around Jack. I grew a

tough exterior to prove to him that I was not afraid. I also began to run for endurance and lift weights to show that I was strong enough to hold my own.

Then, like a switch, Jack turned off his murderous thoughts and became a reasonable and kind husband again.

Fellowship

Jack and I reconnected with our friends from the homeschool group in Texas. We took our families on nature walks and had a few campfire meals together. The fellowship was sweet and I was thankful that Jack had snapped out of his strange behavior. He even considered going back to church. It had been some time since he had allowed any of us to attend church, and the kids and I missed going.

The kids and I were excited to see the shift in Jack's behavior and his zeal return for the things of the Lord. We began to have family devotions and it brought peace to our lives again.

The Sundays that followed would each start with a positive prospect. Jack would announce that we were going to try a new church. The kids and I would be quick to get ready, in case he decided to change his mind at the last minute.

We'd all gather in the car with anticipation, hoping that we would meet new friends to break the cycle of isolation we felt. We longed for stability, but each Sunday brought disappointment. Jack would drive us to church. He would circle the parking lot a few times then announce, "I can't do it. I just can't do it."

This happened for three Sundays in a row with three different churches. On our fourth Sunday, Jack woke up and again told everyone to get ready for church. With reluctance and doubt, we dressed and headed for the door.

Jack drove to the church and pulled up into the parking lot. To my surprise, he and Josiah went inside, while the rest of us waited in the car, as instructed. A few minutes later Jack came back. He slammed the door of the car then vented his frustrations as he cast judgment upon the people of the church.

"I walked into that church and was handed a bulletin, then walked back out," he ranted. "I am so sick of Christians. They are all the same."

I thought quietly about Jack's comment. *If he feels that way about Christians, then he feels that way about the kids and me. Maybe that is why he treats me with resentment and disrespect.*

Jack was fickle about church and never followed through with his desire to go back. I was afraid his heart would turn cold again and we would be back on the road of adversity.

I tried to keep things neutral, since I only had a few months of school left. In spite of that, everything I said was taken the wrong way and Jack negated the neutral in each conversation. He picked fights with me and acted as if we had been in a dispute for weeks.

"Can we be done arguing now?" he'd ask.

With a puzzled look, I would reply, "I wasn't in a fight with you, Jack."

When it was time for bed, Jack created an imaginary line down the center of the bed and forbade me to place my hand or foot over it.

When morning came, he'd greet me with a punch to my nose from his elbow. I became tired of his cross antics and chose to sleep on the couch again, as I'd often done over the last year or two when things would get bad.

As each day passed, Jack complained about how much I studied for school.

He would clear his throat and ask, "Can you be done with that now?"

The tension didn't let up in the days to follow. I couldn't wait for him to leave for work and I dreaded the hour he would return.

Jack met a friend at work and would send her messages every night from the computer. I confronted Jack.

"Are you having an affair?"

"No!" he insisted defensively. "Just because I have had several affairs in the past doesn't mean I'm in another one. You have got to learn to let go of the past and forgive me. 'Jesus said we are to forgive others seventy times seven.'"

I walked away from the heat of Jack's anger and went into another room to think about what he said. *Yes, we are to forgive, and when it says we are to forgive seventy times seven, it means we are to forgive as many times as it takes. However, boundaries are healthy and trust is earned. I shouldn't allow people in my emotionally safe place that I can't trust. Trust and forgiveness are two different things. Matthew 18:21-22 is talking about forgiveness, not trust.*

Sparks of Discernment

Blame-shifting and Twisting Scripture

Abusers often find ways to divert your attention away from the wrong they have done. They will find your faults so that they can blame you, taking your focus off of themselves.

Blame-shifting is an unethical skill that falls under the category of mind games. Quoting scripture is a common tool used by abusers to point out your faults and divert your attention away from their own actions. I will offer you a few ideas for what you can do to combat this fiery dart of spiritual abuse.

1.) Pray for wisdom and ask the Lord to show you the truth.

2.) When someone quotes scripture, always ask for the book, chapter, and verse, so you can look it up. Many times the abuser will pull a phrase out of the Bible and overlook what is said before and after the verse, using it out of context. When they pick out just a phrase or just one verse, it is easier for them to twist the words or meaning to benefit their situation.

3.) Many abusers confuse the victim by misinterpreting a verse that should be clarified with the use of a Bible commentary. Get a commentary and check the meaning of the verse for yourself.

"Each person is tempted when they are dragged away by their own evil desire and enticed. Then after the desire has conceived, it gives birth to sin; and when sin is full-grown, gives birth to death." (James 1:14-15 NIV).

God does not approve of our sin. Eventually we pay for it through death. For a Christian to believe otherwise means that he or she has swallowed the lies of the enemy. Jack was selfish, demeaning, and mean. These characteristics are evidence of a person living in sin. If you do not happen to share my spiritual beliefs, the principle is the same in the secular world-- toxic behaviors and venomous characteristics (what I understand to be an individual living in sin) are damaging to those around the guilty party.

The common lie I have encountered in emotionally abusive homes is that the head of the home can set the rules, even if they are sadistic, immoral, tainted with evil, and infused with mean behavior. The abuser will twist the scriptures to support their belief system, or in non-Christian homes, create their own rationale and rules to govern others. But in reality they have actually deceived themselves.

"Don't be deceived, my dear brothers and sisters, every good and perfect gift is from above, coming down from the Father of lights who does not change like shifting shadows. He chose to give us birth through the Word of truth, that we might be a kind of first-fruits of all He created." (James 1:16-18 NIV).

God's desires are pure and they heal the brokenhearted. Truth brings fruitful living that encourages and uplifts others. Why would God care? Because He loves us and wants to bless us.

Seeing the Cycle

Once again, I outlined Jack's behavior pattern in my mind. The first thing he did was lose control of his anger, then he'd give the silent treatment for a few days. We would tiptoe around him with the hope that we wouldn't set off his anger alarm. Then I would tell him that I was sorry that I made him angry, even if it wasn't my fault, for I knew it was the only way to end the silent treatment.

After a week of emotional upheaval, Jack would switch gears

and quickly climb up the spiritual mountain for three weeks. He would read his Bible, infuse his mind with Christian music, and recommit his life to Christ with what looked like heartfelt dedication. Unfortunately, it never lasted more than three weeks, because the stress and tension of life would build and cause him to slide back down the spiritual mountain. By the end of the third week of his spiritual journey, he would restart his behavior cycle with another fit of rage.

Over the years, I tried to overlook Jack's angry upheavals. The downside of that survival technique caused me to ignore an unhealthy lifestyle that needed guidance and direction. Instead, it manifested into something more dangerous.

Jack made my life miserable on a daily basis. His ugly temper brought me distress and interfered with my ability to concentrate at work, home, and school. The problem left me feeling trapped in a hopeless situation.

Emergency Money

I still trusted Jack to provide for our family financially. Because of this, I lacked the courage to walk away from the mess we were in. I found it easier to trust Jack than to trust God. I had made minimum wage at my salon job and it caused me to doubt my ability to provide for my kids. Because of my insecurity and the fact that I invested sixteen years of my life into our marriage, I chose to give Jack a chance to redeem himself. I had seen God work in his heart before and I knew He could do it again, maybe if I just prayed harder and more frequently.

I opened my Bible and prayed scripture over the difficulties we faced, just as I had done over the past four years. To my surprise, my life did not turn around. Instead, Jack grew more belligerent and unpredictable.

When we moved to Texas, I did it with the hope that our family would receive intervention, but that plan seemed to be failing.

I looked for another counselor but Jack refused to participate. I called my parents out of desperation and asked for advice.

"You are the one who needs to make the choice to leave Jack," my mother said. "If I come down there and pull you out of that mess, you will run right back into his arms."

The conversation with my mom ended with a final note of encouragement.

"Shelly," she said. "I have mailed you a cell phone and two hundred dollars to help you and the kids escape, when you're ready."

I knew I couldn't hide the cell phone from Jack so I told him a fib.

"Jack, my parents mailed me a cell phone so the kids can contact me on the days I'm at school."

Jack grew angry. "I can never give you the right things to keep your parents happy. I don't know why they think you need a cell phone."

Jack's anger was so strong, I felt it necessary to write a two-page letter that explained why I feared he might kill me. The letter also revealed where he would most likely hide my body.

I walked down to the salon where I worked and asked my co-workers to keep the letter in the company safe. I instructed them to give it to the police if I ever came up missing.

Sparks of Discernment

A Cry for Help

It is not uncommon for a victim of abuse to write a letter when they feel they are in danger. When they offer the warning to a friend or relative, the receiver should immediately give it to the police for documentation, and offer to take their friend to see a counselor.

A letter is a cry for help. Many times the victim doesn't have the courage to give it to the police themselves because they don't feel there is enough evidence to favor their side of the story.

Help from Jack

I was physically exhausted and struggled to keep my eyes open as my daily stressors increased.

I worked hard to fulfill Jack's expectations while I desperately tried to finish school. I felt burnt out and decided to humble myself and ask Jack for help.

"Jack, we need to talk."

Jack grabbed a chair from the table and threw it in the middle of the kitchen floor, then straddled it with the back of the chair facing me. With cold and calculated eyes, he shot a death stare in my direction.

"Here I am, talk to me now!" Anger filled the room as he shouted. "What exactly do you want from me?"

I turned away from Jack and calmly answered, "I supported you while you went to school numerous times, and now that I'm in school, I need your help."

"I'm right here, right now!" Jack emitted arrogance as he tried to intimidate me with his dark tone. "Tell me what you want me to do."

I looked at Jack, then turned back toward the stove while I broke the spaghetti noodles in half and placed them in the steamy, hot water.

"Jack, I need you to do more than just help me right this second. I need you to do a few chores around the house until I finish school," I said. "You come home every night after work and plant your face in front of the computer and TV. It would help me a great deal if you would pick up a pizza or put dinner in the oven for me."

Jack's eyes danced with fire as he jumped up with anger and yelled, "I will not do that!"

He stood up, then abruptly threw his chair back in place at the kitchen table before leaving the room.

I turned to look at the windowsill where the tiny vase of plastic lavender flowers sat. I recalled the words that my messenger from Grawn, Michigan had spoken, "I know it's the Lord's will for you to move back to Texas."

The words that she'd spoken confused me. The only thing I

was certain of, was that the plastic flowers in the tiny clay vase had melted from the swelter of the Texas sun the same way my soul melted from the heat of Jack's anger.

After all my prayers, how could this be God's will? I asked myself.

Power and Control

Knock, knock, knock.

I opened the front door of the house and there stood our neighbor, Miss May. She asked if she could talk to Jack and me. Both of us stepped outside to listen to Miss May's concerns.

"The trees in your front yard are going to fall on my car and I need you to chop them down."

Jack lengthened his stance and answered Miss May with belligerence, "No!"

Miss May was not happy and began to argue with Jack. Then she turned to look at me.

"You are being abused by this man," she said. "I have watched how he treats y'all and he is abusive!"

May walked toward Jack and stood up to him like I had never seen anybody do. I was so pleased! He had finally met his match. To make the situation worse for him, it was with a woman.

Jack had a deep-seated hate for women who spoke out with strong voices and stood against a man's authority. He was a firm believer that women should never be allowed to voice their opinions or give commands.

Jack yelled at the kids and me, "Come on, get back in the house!"

Forcible Violation

The kids ran to their rooms. I made my way to the family room with Jack right behind me. He then yelled, "Sit down on the couch right now!"

Jack started a rant that gradually gained momentum then mutated into yelling, and eventually screaming.

"No woman has any authority to talk to me in that manner," he yelled emphatically. "I do not know who she thinks she is, but she should not concern herself with how I treat you and the kids!"

Jack's face turned red as he stood tall and displayed tension and strength. He continued to scream. "I am not abusive and she has no right to accuse me of that type of behavior!"

I curled up in a ball and cried. The intensity of Jack's anger made me feel threatened as his rage grew. "I am not yelling at you. I am angry that Miss May thinks she can talk to me that way!"

The momentum of Jack's tirade culminated into a flash of power and control against me. Suddenly I was pinned up against the couch and taken advantage of by force. The whole scene happened faster than I could respond. I froze in my moment of fear and was unable to process the destruction that had just been committed against me.

Jack left the room. I sat in a state of shock as I stared off in the distance. I had been denied the act of marriage for many months, and now Jack had chosen to display himself before me with a force of selfishness. I felt violated, dirty, and used.

Sparks of Discernment

Validating Sexual Abuse Trauma

When I was living in Texas in 2007, I was told that sexual assault survivors need to have said "no," in order for the assault to be considered rape. However, when I interviewed retired police officer of California Mike Zannitto, he mentioned that there are so many other factors to consider with sexual assault. He encouraged me to do a search on California Penal Code 261 PC, and to read all the subsections that are outlined on what is legally considered as sexual assault. What I found was encouraging and I wish more states had similar laws. Look into the laws in your state to learn more about your rights and what actions to take to improve your chances of finding justice. One thing Mr. Zannitto stressed was to be sure to mention when you give your report that you tried to fend off your perpetrator.

I asked Mr. Zannitto what would be the best way to go about reporting a sexual assault when the victim is in a relationship with the perpetrator. His advice was to go to the doctor for an exam right away. If necessary, give the perpetrator a medical reason for your doctor's visit such as your cycle has been off or it hurts when you use the restroom. Disclose to the doctor what happened with your abuser. They will do an exam to look for things such as tears and bruising.

I share this with you because there are so many different scenarios in which I found myself that I just didn't know my rights, even as a married woman. I was concerned that no one would believe me when my abuser sexually violated me and I wasn't even sure if what had happened was considered to be sexual assault. Even if you are not sure, file a report right away, and be ready to press charges in some cases. Immediate action after the assault is essential, so that as much physical evidence can be recorded as possible. It will be difficult. But it is a crucial first step toward healing and removing yourself from a dangerous situation.

It is vital that you see a counselor when you have been sexually violated. If you wait too long, then you begin to question what happened. You could end up minimizing your trauma with thoughts that trick you into believing that you, the victim, were wrong. The problem with that is, even if your mind no longer registers it as rape, your body will still have triggers, which means that you have buried it deep into your subconscious. This complicates the healing process, and makes it more difficult to prove wrongdoing in a court of law. Remember, just because the law may seem to favor the perpetrator (for example, by requiring the victim to have said "no"), this does not mean that your abuser's actions were justified or acceptable in any way.

You deserve justice, you deserve respect, and you deserve safety.

Obstacle Course

My stress and fear left me sleepless as each ungodly event

unveiled itself.

When I slept, I hallucinated with dreams of pink and blue sea monsters. They would try to reach up over my bed and take me down under the sea with them.

I knew I just needed a few days of rest but I could not seem to catch a break.

The breeze outside blew the hot summer air through the wind chimes. Their song beckoned me to grab a pillow and rest on the family room floor.

I lay in front of the sliding glass door and allowed my tired, achy body to meld into the floor beneath me. The cool air from the ceiling fan whipped across my bare feet, while the warm Texas wind blew on my face. I closed my eyes tight and begged for the melody of the chimes to lull me into a deep slumber, but to no avail.

I was satisfied when I slept for a few hours the following night. But when I woke, I was frazzled and had no will to get out of bed. The smile I carried on my face and in my heart disappeared.

I lay in bed with my hands reaching up to the heavens to praise the Lord that I was still alive. I then reached for the window blinds that were placed over my head and peeked out at the sunny sky. Immediately, I sat up with worry as I realized that I could not feel the segments on the blinds. I applied more pressure and again ran my hands down the accordion style blinds. My anxiety grew. I still could not feel the jump from one segment of the blinds to the next. I stood up to confirm that I was not stuck in a bad dream. I then ran my hands up and down the stucco wall and discovered that I still had no sensation in my fingers or hands.

I became troubled and ran outside to wake up my senses on nature's obstacle course. With my bare feet, I walked across the heavily-pebbled flagstone path that led out to our patio. I expected my knees to buckle under the pain of the tiny pebbles that were embedded into the bottom of my feet. Instead, I became anxious and fearful because I felt nothing. I then made my way to the rough crabgrass. I slowly traveled over it with the hope that I would feel the prick of the grass on the bottom of my feet, or take in the cold sensation of the morning dew. Next, I ran over to a little mud hole and squished the cold earth between my toes. My feet were still numb and devoid of any sensation.

I felt as if my body was in an unrealistic shell and I lived on the outside of it. I still had control of where my body went and what it did, but I felt nothing.

My emotions were just as numb as my body. I couldn't cry and I couldn't laugh. I then recalled the conversation with my kids on the issue of cutting. We had talked about how some people cut their own skin in an unhealthy attempt to reassure themselves that they are alive and capable of feeling. Determined to find that reassurance in a healthy way rather than resorting to self-harm, I ran my quickly-improvised obstacle course again to regain sensation to my feet and hands.

I continued the obstacle course, hoping that my emotions would also return. Instead, I became panic-stricken with the idea that my mind could possibly shut down.

I will not let Jack win this game, I thought. *I will get my feeling back.*

I became consumed with the exercise and chose to run the course repeatedly. I was elated when I finally regained all sensation to both my hands and feet. However, my emotions were still numb from Jack's angry outburst, and my heart was empty of compassion. The only compassion I had in reserve was for my children and my family in Michigan. I could trust them and knew

I was safe with them.

I thought I could preserve my sanity until I finished school. My plan was to push through my chaotic lifestyle and put up an emotional wall to shield me from Jack's spite and malice.

That same evening, after everybody went to bed, I stepped outside to sit in the car. I popped in a CD to listen to the lyrics of a song, *Praise You In This Storm*. I was devoid of any emotion and unable to reach deep into my soul to pull out a praise for the Lord. The music had no effect. It didn't cheer me up nor did it encourage me. I turned the radio louder with the expectation that it would move me to compassion.

As the music played, I began to think about the Holy Trinity. I knew and understood the love of God and I comprehended that Jesus died on the cross for my sins. Still, I knew that I had missed something important in my relationship with Christ. I had felt the same void many times in my life. Just then, the song changed on the CD player to *Father, Spirit, Jesus*.

Finally, it clicked in my head. The Holy Spirit had held back His blessings from my life because I had extinguished Him in my time of sorrow. I stepped out of the car with a renewed hope and allowed the Holy Spirit to be my benefactor in my time of desperation. **(John 16:7-13)**

Sparks of Discernment

Cutting

Cutting is a health hazard that is not a productive way to handle stress, relationship issues, abuse, natural disasters, or any other problem. Although teens and adults alike have resorted to this unhealthy and addictive coping mechanism, I want you to know that there are healthier options that can be achieved with the help of a trained counselor. There can be a successful outcome if the client follows through with the techniques as they address their past hurts and disappointments.

Instead of hurting yourself, it is important to work with a professional who can pull out the past damage that has brought you to this point. You are important, and self-harm doesn't achieve positive results.

Webster's Dictionary describes respect as a means to recognize the worth of a person. Abusive influences cause the victim to offer respect to the abuser and others but not to themselves. In fact, many victims talk down about themselves to others. Instead, victims need to discover their self-worth and offer their bodies respect by doing what they can to not allow themselves to be put in harm's way, and by not inflicting injury on themselves.

SEVENTEEN

MAY DAY, MAY DAY

We celebrated Jack's birthday in July of 2007. Jack made no effort to connect with me in spite of all the energy I spent to make his special day happen. In fact, he moved ten feet away from me when I sat next to him.

While he opened his gifts, I remained planted in my own thoughts and reflected on the events that had brought us back to Texas.

Where did things go wrong in our relationship?

I could never come to any conclusion. Every time I thought about it, the thoughts just looped around into one big continuous circle with no end and no answer.

I had lost two emotional boxing matches to Jack, one in Iowa and the other in Texas. Now, twelve years later, I was faced with a third boxing match. Each morning a new round started with the sound of the alarm clock.

I struggled to complete the required hours for school while I endured Jack's ill-treatment. Exhausted and worn down, I could hardly keep my weary eyes open. Finally, I decided to surrender and throw in my sweat-drenched towel. The only problem was convincing Jack that quitting school was a good idea.

Jack and I sat down in the family room for a heart-to-heart conversation. However, against my wishes, he invited the kids in.

I looked up at him. "Jack, let the kids go play," I said. "This needs to be handled between us adults."

"No," Jack replied. "If you have something to say, I want everybody to hear it."

"OK, fine. I want to quit school."

Jack stood to prepare himself for the fight. He snorted and paced the floor like a bull, moving from one side to the other. I watched as he meditated on which emotional punch he should deliver first.

"What?" He finally let loose, shouting. "Why do you think you have the right to quit school and where is this idea coming from?"

I stood and shifted my weight from one foot to the other as I prepared to defend myself from his next emotional blow.

"I can't live like this anymore," I said. "I am exhausted with the workload of school and all the house chores. Most of all, I miss how things used to be. We never have family time anymore and I really miss the kids. I feel as if they have suffered the most in this situation."

Jack became enraged. "First of all, the kids will be fine. They do not need you as their mother anymore!" His anger crescendoed as he spat out each word. "Second of all, you will not quit school! I refuse to pay your school bill with nothing to show for it. You will go back to work and pay your fair share of the bills after you graduate."

I hovered over the ropes of the emotional boxing ring as I tried to recover from Jack's heartless words. I decided that the rest of our conversation needed to happen without the kids around. "Jack, meet me in the bedroom."

I sat at the foot of the bed. Jack distanced himself from me, sitting by the headboard. I took in a deep breath as I buckled under the pressure and slid off the bed to take in the cool comfort of the wooden floor beneath my body. I sobbed as I threw my first emotional punch back at him. "I can't believe that I have come to this point. I want out of this marriage for good. Jack, I want a divorce."

Jack sat stunned. I had knocked his head a little too hard with my words. I waited for him to respond.

"What?!" Jack squealed in a high-pitched voice. "Why do you want a divorce?"

"I don't want to live life like this anymore. You are mean to me, and you have made my life miserable, and you still won't help me out around the house."

"I don't understand where you are coming from," Jack said. "I think we just need to take a few days off so you can sort things out. A divorce is not the answer for a less miserable life."

I cried. I felt trapped in a life of misery with a hateful man. It left me depressed, with a heart full of sorrow.

The next morning I returned to my usual routine. When I

looked in the mirror, the evidence of sorrow was written on my face. My eyes were puffy from the tears I shed the night before. I ran out to the kitchen and opened the freezer door to grab the two spoons I kept in there for these tearful occasions. They weren't there. I must have used them earlier in the week and forgot to replace them. I couldn't remember. The whole week had been a big blur of sadness.

I grabbed a couple of ice cubes instead and placed them on my eyelids to reduce the swelling. With an anxious spirit, I lay on my bed for twenty minutes and prayed.

I walked back to the mirror to check my eyes. The ice cubes hadn't helped. I knew another twenty minutes was needed but there wasn't time. Instead, I grabbed my makeup bag as I heard my inner voice speak. *Shelly, take what you have learned from school about makeup and cover your swollen face. Make yourself look good.*

I stared at myself in the mirror in silence. *Am I covering up my wounds just as a battered woman does?*

I pushed the thought away and hurried to get ready for school.

I walked into class ten minutes late. I lowered my head and allowed my hair to cover my face, hiding from any onlookers. The words that tore my soul apart the night before left me to dangle in a sea of hopelessness that I could not see my way out of.

I struggled to process the information from class and knew I needed to reach out for help. Desperate for a solution, I went to the finance department at school to see what my options would be if I continued my education in Michigan. I was distraught to hear that my college credits were non-transferable.

School let out and I made it home before Jack did. I searched the internet for information on emotional abuse. I found nothing.

Was emotional abuse even recognized as a type of abuse? What were the characteristics and the signs, and what options were offered to help those who were in an emotionally abusive situation?

Can I make life with Jack work for three more months? Would it be worth leaving Texas with a school bill and no cosmetology license?

Jack's oppression was thick and my future looked bleak. Discouraged about my meeting with the finance department, I gave up and didn't show up for school. I didn't call and I didn't care.

Sparks of Discernment

Self-defense

I felt like a boxer on a losing streak, with my opponent being the victor in each emotional fight. He threw the most powerful punches he knew. I had learned through research that small fighters could still overcome larger opponents with the right techniques, but I had no confidence in myself and I felt powerless. In spite of what I'd learned, I saw it as an impossible feat to beat the Undefeated

Champion of Emotional Abuse.

I had no strategy to follow because I didn't have a trainer to show me the ropes on how to navigate my way through the murky trials of emotional abuse. In the end, I lost everything except my faith and my life.

Boxers are trained with strategies on how to fight in a boxing match. First they think about the punches they will use, then they practice them. A victim also needs to have her or his strategy in place in case she or he is attacked by an abuser.

Tim Larkin is a self-defense expert and the author of *Survive the Unthinkable: A Total Guide to Women's Self-Protection*. He also co-wrote *How to Survive the Most Critical 5 Seconds of Your Life* with self-defense instructor Chris Ranck-Buhr. Both of these books go into detail about how an individual can defeat, or at least escape from, any person intending to cause them harm, using techniques that might not be considered "fair" in the boxing ring, such as a shot to the eyes or throat. What you need to remember in a situation with your abuser is that the fight is already unfair. Your goal is to get away and survive, and it can be done.

Crash

Jack never softened his heart, but because of my emotional state, I had no choice but to trust him. I felt impoverished, with a vulnerable heart of a child, and hoped I would not get hit with another emotional blow.

I could no longer produce enough energy to stand steady on my feet. My strength had left me, though my will to live was stable and strong. I looked into Jack's eyes, searching for a measure of mercy. I yearned for him to handle my feeble spirit and weak body with care.

I sat on the couch, worried about my condition. "Jack, I can't sleep."

He opened a box and handed me a pill.

"What is it?" I asked.

"It's a sleeping pill," he answered. Though there was still daylight, he probably thought it would help me relax enough for a nap.

"Let me see the box for myself."

Jack willingly handed me the package. I looked inside to be sure all the pills matched then popped it in my mouth while I read the directions. Anxiety suddenly took over my body when I realized the pill was not compatible with my untreated hypertension.

Jack had refused me the right to be seen by a doctor for my high blood pressure. I tried to manage it through diet and exercise but the stress I was under ruled over my healthy choices.

My heart began to beat through the walls of my chest as I gasped for air.

"What is the matter with you?" Jack yelled.

I spoke with fear in my voice, "You gave me this pill and after

I read the warning label, I realized that I should not have taken it. I have high blood pressure, Jack. My reading has been 220/180. I'm scared and I think I'm going to die."

"Settle down!" Jack hollered, clearly annoyed. "You will be okay if you stop thinking about it! You need to stop fighting the effects of the pill and relax, so you can sleep!"

My mind went spinning into overdrive as I thought about my blood pressure crisis. *I took the pill. I think this is it. My life has come to an end and I'm not sure I will ever wake up again.*

I was amazed to open my eyes thirteen hours later. However, I was unable to raise my hands to the heavens to praise God, because my body would not move with the commands of my mind. Sleep overtook me once again.

On the second day of my crash, I slept on and off. Jack had set up an air mattress in the middle of the den, and this is where my exhausted body desperately attempted to rest and recover. When I woke, my mind was quiet and my body was immovable until the sun went down. That was when Jack served me a quarter of a cup of rice and a quarter of a cup of peas. He then handed me four ounces of water with which to wash it down. Suddenly, I became ravenously hungry after I finished my small meal.

"Jack, can I have more to eat?"

"No, you have had enough to eat for now," he said.

My strength was gone and I could not muster any to lift myself from the air mattress to refill my plate myself.

After my meal, Jack spoke with nervousness. "My parents came by today to see if they could help. I told them that I had everything under control."

I scoffed under my breath, "That's because you're trying to hide what you've done to me."

Jack had been making sure that the kids were fed while I was immobile, but because he felt that that already exceeded his duties, he'd parked them in front of video games and the computer to minimize any parenting responsibilities. He was frustrated that it now fell to him to take the kids to their lawn mowing jobs. When I woke on the third day, the house was quiet, but it wasn't long before I heard the familiar sounds of my children arriving home. As the boys ran through the front door from mowing lawns, they quickly made their way to me with concern in their eyes. My heart was glad to see them. I wanted to talk to them but Jack quickly intercepted, shooing the boys out of the way.

Jack hunched over me on his hands and knees and shook the air mattress as he screamed in my face. "When are you going to get up out of this bed and finally do your part around this house? I have done nothing but cook and clean while your worthless body has laid here and done nothing!"

I managed to get myself off of the air mattress and slowly crawled along the floor, dragging my weak body up to the couch four feet away from where I had lain. After I sat up, I looked down at myself and noticed that I was still dressed in the same clothes that I had been wearing three days ago. Just then I realized that I needed to use the restroom, something I hadn't done in days.

I stood up gradually and felt as if I had been drugged. I held my body up along the wall as I slowly walked to the bathroom at the other end of the house. Eventually, I made my way back to the couch in the living room.

I heard low chatter behind me and turned to look. There I spotted my three children as they peeked around the corner to check on me. After a few seconds, Jack spotted them and commanded them to leave the room.

My spirit lifted in the few seconds that I was allowed to look into their anxious eyes of concern. Joy revived my heart and it gave me a renewed hope that my life with Jack would end, and the kids and I would someday live in peace.

I knew that Jack's ultimate motive was to keep the kids separated from me and break any bonds we had. This became obvious with his reaction when Samantha dashed back into the room and quickly knelt down in front of my bare feet with a bottle of nail polish.

"Hey, I told you to go!" Jack yelled.

Samantha stood up to speak, in spite of the fear in her eyes. "I was just going to polish her toes."

Jack hesitated, then shook his head no. Then he abruptly changed his mind and gave Samantha the approval she waited for. Humbly and quietly, Samantha shared her deepest gratitude of compassion for me with an act of servitude, just as Mary did when she washed Jesus's feet in **John 12:3**.

EIGHTEEN

EXTINGUISHING THE FLAME OF INDIGNATION

*J*ack's aggression continued for many days after my meltdown. I laid lifelessly on the couch while he constantly badgered me.

"What are you going to change in your life so that this doesn't happen again? I need you to function at full capacity if you're going to live in this house."

I caught the first few words he said, but my mind was unable to comprehend all that came out of his mouth. Even though my thought process was distracted and foggy, I came up with an answer to Jack's question, to get him off my back.

"I need to read my Bible more and take notes so I don't disappoint you," I mumbled.

"Okay, show me what you did for today," he demanded.

Jack talked down to me, verbally disciplining me like he had done with the kids. His tone said it all-- he didn't think I could think for myself or find my own way.

"I read the verse, 'Jesus wept,' " I answered.

Written words had recently become difficult for me to comprehend, but I clearly understood those two words. I, too, had wept for many months as I prayed and asked God to show His mercy on my family.

Jack's lips moved around on his face as he thought about my answer. "And how is that supposed to help you be a better wife?"

I held my breath for a moment because I wasn't sure of the right answer. I let out a deep sigh. "Obviously I need to be more sensitive to your needs."

"Okay, I guess that's a start," he said hesitantly, as he stood up. He backed away from me, then returned to his computer game before he commented, "You're not off the hook. You need to think about this a little longer."

But all I could do was sleep.

My ability to function was temporarily out of order and I was unable to account for many of the days that had passed me by. However, I began to recover, with a renewed spirit that caused Jack to hate me even more.

A month later, I regained my strength and was thankful that I could finally grasp the words on a page. I took the opportunity to read my Bible more, with the hope that I would find the answers I needed for my dilemma.

My head hurt from the tears I shed over the realization that God's solution to my problem was different than what I had prayed for. I always prayed to the Lord as if He were a genie in a bottle. I expected Him to do what I thought was best for my life, and when He didn't give me the answer I wished for, I doubted Him. I was left to wonder why God wouldn't make Jack follow His laws and I couldn't figure out why my family was spiritually under siege.

In the last days of July in 2007, I discovered that Jack had brought home some fantasy books for the kids to look through. They made me nervous, because Jack had told me early in our marriage that when he was in high school, he became deeply involved with the same books and struggled to separate himself from the acts of violence the books alluded to. He told me he had to quit reading them because he was tempted to carry out the cruel acts of behavior. Because of this, I didn't understand what his purpose was for introducing them to the kids.

"Why have you brought these ungodly books into our home?" I asked.

Jack tried to negotiate a compromise with me. "The books are pretty harmless at first, but don't worry, I'll help them keep the fantasy world separate from their reality. I won't let them read the books without me."

I became irate. "What are you thinking? All these years, you have been dogmatic about not allowing our family to watch horror movies, or read anything that encouraged violent behavior, and now you bring this into our home? What is wrong with you?"

Jack turned his back on me and threw his hands up in the air as he walked away.

A few days later, curiosity got the best of Peter. He rifled through Jack's books looking for the first book in the fantasy series, then ran to hide.

Peter was gone a bit too long and it caused Jack to check and see if he had swiped one of the new books. Sure enough, the first book in the series had disappeared.

"Where is my first book from the fantasy series?" Jack's bellow resonated throughout the house.

Fear overtook Peter's face as he swallowed. "I- I have it."

"What?" he yelled. "I have told you that those books were not for your eyes, unless I'm with you. Why have you done this?"

Peter's eyes began to well up with tears. "I was just curious and wanted to find out more about it."

Jack began to rant with unreasonable nonsense. I looked around and noticed that I wasn't the only one who tuned him out. I spoke up.

"Why did you bring these fantasy books into the home in the first place?" I asked. "You're just creating temptation for the kids to fall into, and I will not allow this to go on."

Later that evening, I discovered that Jack downloaded a war game on the computer that also encouraged violent behavior. Because of the stress I was feeling, I needed some fresh air so I stepped outside to walk the trash out to the dumpster. I opened the lid, then stood in complete silence as I gazed at the horror that was before my eyes.

Jack had thrown out boxes and boxes of Bibles as well as Biblical commentaries and study aids.

My heart grew sick as I thought about the violence he was suddenly adamant about adding to our home and his desire to push the things of God out of our home. Then my mind went on to all the missionaries that begged for donations of old Bibles. Suddenly, I had a strong urge to dive in and rescue them from the bottom of the dumpster so that they could be put to good use. Instead, I marched back into the house and immediately confronted Jack.

"What have you done?"

"What are you talking about?" Jack responded.

"Why have you thrown out all your Bible books?"

Jack looked surprised that I dared to ask. "I don't need them anymore," he said. "And they took up too much space on my bookshelf. If it's any comfort, I kept a few of my books. Go ahead and look on my shelf."

"You're done with God, aren't you?" I said. "That would explain why you treat me with disrespect and have influenced the kids to walk down a dark path of violence. I will not have it!"

The next day after Jack left for work, I became irrational and did the unthinkable. I walked our new computer out to the dumpster and threw it in, to get the point across to Jack that I would not give my consent on allowing violence in the home. Because of my actions, it was the end of any existing love that Jack may have had left for me.

I disapproved of the godless path that Jack decided to lead our family down, and knew that it would now be my sole responsibility to pass down the Christian faith to our children.

When Jack found out that I had thrown his new computer in the garbage, he persecuted me. I stood against him and quoted our family verse, "But as for me and my house, we will serve the Lord." **(Joshua 24:15b KJV)**. Jack didn't care what I had to say. His words and actions toward me worsened over the coming days.

I didn't know what to do. I needed guidance, and didn't know where to turn. One afternoon, I sat down in front of the window and opened my Bible to **Job 19:7-8**, then paused for a moment. I realized that I could relate to Job when he screamed out to God for help and was given no justice. Job said, "God has blocked my way so I cannot pass; He has covered my paths with darkness." **(Job 19:8).**

I felt that my family was dying a spiritual death and there was no justice done to stop Jack from his mean-spirited ways. I prayed, "God, change my husband."

I paused to look over at my piano where a handwritten verse on an index card sat. Stella and Wayne had shared the verse with Jack, to give him encouragement before our move to Texas.

> " 'I know the plans I have for you,' declares the Lord, 'plans to prosper you and not to harm you, plans to give you hope and a future.' " **(Jeremiah 29:11 NIV).**

I read the verse. It brought me no emotional relief, nor did it make sense. The trauma from Jack's emotional abuse was now permanently etched into the history of our family timeline, and it no longer lined up with the verse I read. I examined the situation I was in and could not see brightness or hope for my future. All I saw was a dark path of evil demise.

I returned to read more out of my Bible, "He has taken away my honor and removed the crown from my head. He beats me down on every side until I am gone; He destroys my hope like a fallen tree." **(Job 19: 9-10).**

Because I had thrown Jack's computer in the dumpster and because of my Biblical convictions, I'd lost the respect of my husband and my in-laws. I had lost my crown of honor and was rejected and forgotten. Jack had turned into a vulture and I was his prey. He shred me to pieces as he destroyed my character and stripped me of my dignity and self-worth to those we associated with. With each passing day, the intensity of Jack's emotional attacks had been increasing. As a result of Jack's persistence, the Lord pressed upon my heart to ask for help from the deacons of the church.

I waited for Jack to arrive home from work. When I heard the car pull up in the driveway, I walked outside to meet him.

"Jack," I said. "I want you to know that I'm going to invite the deacons of the church over."

"What?" he screamed. "You didn't call them yet, did you?! You have no right to invite them to dinner to help us! What I do with this family is my business and they have no right to tell me what to do!"

We took our conversation into the house. Jack commanded me to sit at the table, then rebuked my actions with disgust. For the next two hours, he expressed how much he resented my existence. He then slammed his Bible down on the kitchen table and protested against my idea, while he excused his own sinful behavior. I couldn't take it any longer. My mind blocked out his angry voice and all I could focus on was the rate of speed at which his lips moved, as he gnashed his teeth and snarled at me.

My hope to revive our family was squashed. I walked away from Jack and sat in my room. My heart filled with sorrow as I mentally shaved my head out of sadness, tore my clothes, and sat in ashes, just like Job did in **Job 1:20**. I grieved over the loss of our Christian heritage and the lack of godly influence on my precious family.

Sparks of Discernment

Keeping Track of Behavior

The mistrust from Jack's previous actions caused me to evaluate his behavior. I came to the conclusion that I should've recorded all of his strange and hostile actions from the past. If I had done this, I would have seen that there were deadly and abusive patterns throughout our relationship. A chart would have proved that Jack had an unhealthy abusive cycle that needed attention, and it would have given me the evidence I needed to make better choices for the kids and for myself.

Many frown on the act of keeping track of another person's behavior, because it may seem as if one is trying to keep score. To forgive and forget means to put it behind you when someone apologizes. Unfortunately, there are some who abuse the forgive-and-forget rule.

Throughout the Old Testament of the Bible, the Lord recalls how the Israelites repeatedly struggled with selfish ambitions, disobedience, lust, greed, idol worship, and so on. Moses confronted them about those issues. They confessed, changed their ways, then repeated the same offenses over again. Because of their sin they were not allowed to enter the Promised Land. **(Exodus Chapter 3 through Joshua 24:29)**.

When or if your spouse repeats their offenses, you must confront them with a pastor or counselor, for accountability. A pastor or counselor can also help you follow through with consequences for the abuser.

Ultimatum

I was fed up with the way Jack treated me, so I sought justice. I stood with the strength of a Clydesdale horse, setting new standards and expecting Jack to play by my rules.

After Jack left for work on the third Thursday of the month, I collected our social security cards and our immunization and legal records, and placed them on Jack's dresser. I then topped the peak of the pile with our wedding rings. I pulled the suitcases from the attic and packed enough clothes for the kids and myself. Next I called Jack at work.

He answered, "This is Jack."

I wanted Jack to know that I would no longer tolerate his mean-spirited ways, so I spoke with a cocky, dominant voice, "Yeah, it's me, your wife."

Jack cheerfully responded as if there had been no tension in our marriage. "What's up?"

"I packed the suitcases for the kids and me, and we are prepared to leave you! If you care about our marriage, come home and we will see if we can work this out."

Twenty minutes later, Jack walked in the door and humbly listened as I threatened to take the kids and leave if he didn't get some help.

I was confident that I had Jack's full attention. "You must stop treating everybody in this family as if we are subservient to you," I said. "And quit yelling at us for every little thing we do or don't do."

"I feel like I am losing control of my whole family," Jack blurted out. "Everybody is becoming independent. You had started going to school, and the kids have started to mow lawns, and I have no control over my family!"

His voice softened as he spoke, "Okay, I will see a counselor and change, so our home will be emotionally and physically safe."

I returned to cosmetology school in the month of August, hopeful that there would be a difference in Jack. After a week, I fell to my knees and went into a constant mindset of prayer, "Lord, I'm confused. I know You are telling me to leave Jack, but what You are saying contradicts what the church has taught me about divorce. I know You can move this mountain and change Jack, but I also know that Jack will not listen to Your direction. How much grace do I give him and how long do I wait for him to make the necessary changes?"

By the second week of August in 2007, I still had no answer from the Lord. I became frustrated and took matters into my own hands.

Jack had been involved with several affairs in the past and I was positive he already had my replacement lined up. I was tired of his unfaithfulness, and just once I wanted him to hurt the same way he hurt me. I wanted to shock him in a way that would cause him to turn his face from his heinous lifestyle and immoral ways. I thought it would be good for him to know how awful it felt to be cheated on.

In the days to follow, I began to dwell on the story about how Abraham had lied to Abimelech in Genesis, Chapter 20. In the end, Abraham walked away blessed. I decided to make the same gutsy move as Abraham, and rang the bell to add another round to our emotional boxing match. I started with a hard punch to the side as I lied to him, "Jack, I'm having an affair."

Jack's face flushed. He stood up and silently left to visit his parents.

My pride and injured spirit rejoiced over how successfully my plan had seemed to work, and I was positive that the lie would cause him to snap out of his belligerent ways.

A few hours later, Jack pulled into the driveway and walked up to me with a broken spirit. He held out his arms and hugged me.

"I want to work things out with you," he said.

Contest

In the third week of August 2007, I received a call from my mom.

"Shelly," she began excitedly. "I entered a Mother's Day contest through our Christian radio station and I won! I want to invite you and two of my sisters to attend a women's conference in Denver, Colorado. Your airfare, hotel, and meals have been paid for by the radio station!"

I wanted to cry. I hadn't seen my mother since things had gotten worse after our move back to Texas. I needed a break from Jack's negativity, and I longed to be refreshed by others who loved the Lord. I choked back the tears as I told my mother, "Yes, Mom, that would be awesome!"

I was aware that God wanted me to focus my attention on my relationship with Him and to look beyond the black hole of despair I was in. I was confident that He wouldn't let me down, and that the answers I needed to my problems would be unlocked through the messages that the speakers would deliver at the conference.

I stepped outside, where Jack was.

"Jack, Mom won an all-expenses-paid trip for four people to a women's conference in Denver, Colorado and she chose me to go with her."

Jack looked down at the grass and quickly paced the length of the backyard, then walked back in my direction. He pursed his lips together as he nodded his head in agreement, "Alright, I'll let you go."

I stood in shock. *Let me go? I didn't ask if I could go.*

I quickly disregarded how Jack answered me, and was glad he had chosen not to go to war with me over the conference.

Denver

In September of 2007, I walked off the plane and took a taxi to my hotel in Denver, where I met up with my mother and two aunts. Just as I opened the car door, my mother attempted to bolt into traffic to get to me. Each sister grabbed an arm to hold her back from being hit by oncoming traffic.

I walked over to her tear-stained face and held her tightly as I listened to what she had to say.

"Oh my gosh, daughter, I am so glad you made it," she said. "I believe God has ordained this event for you, and you will be blessed."

"Mom, this is our special time together and I do not want to talk about my issues with Jack," I told her.

She agreed not to make Jack the focus of our weekend. We then grabbed our luggage and went in to settle into our hotel room. Later that evening, we left for the Friday evening conference session.

The Lord began to soften my heart with the message from the first night. I knew I needed to share what Jack had put me through, and I knew I needed to seek wisdom. Once the evening conference was through, we walked to a little corner coffee shop. I began to share the details of Jack's temper and how it affected me physically and emotionally.

My mother sipped her coffee. She set it down in front of her as she tried to hold back her tears.

"Mom, are you okay?" I asked, knowing it was a lot to process.

She sat silent for a few more minutes before replying. "I'm in shock," she said. "I didn't know it was that bad. I am so upset with Jack, because he promised me that he would take good care of you while you lived in Texas. I'm just mad and I don't know what else to say."

We both sipped our coffee and watched the busy corner of the coffee shop in the evening light.

"Shelly, I need to tell you that when you were back home in Michigan, I noticed that you regressed socially from one holiday season to the next," my mother shared her concern. "You seemed to pull back from everyone and struggled to be your usual happy, outgoing self. Jack's salvation experience happened, and your need to heal was overlooked. He has mistreated you for many years. Plus, you were traumatized by the first six years of your marriage. Now you have explained the most recent things that have happened, and all I can think about is how it has complicated your issues."

I didn't like what my mother had to say, but I knew she was right. We both sat quietly for a moment, then she shared a final thought.

"Shelly, your road of recovery is going to be a long and rough one."

We woke up on Saturday morning with anticipation of what the speakers had to say. I listened to our favorite speaker, Beth Moore, as she opened her Bible and began to share what was on her heart. She explained that we needed to accept our normal and be content with it rather than dream for a bigger, better, or different life. I thought, *Lord have mercy on me. Please tell me that I don't have to stay with Jack and that I don't have to accept the way he treats me.* Then Beth finished her thought. "We need to open our hearts and listen for what the Lord has for each of us, in our own particular situation."

My ears and heart were in tune with what I heard, and I relaxed as she continued to speak. "A woman who is being mistreated is not being treated in a way that is honoring to the Lord."

My head immediately cleared from the message that the church had taught me my whole life, which was to pray and wait for God to change my husband. I was afraid that if I waited on Jack to change, I would not survive to see another Christmas.

Beth continued, "Abuse interferes with the effectiveness of doing the Lord's work because we become consumed and obsessed with the abuse, and it leaves us with no energy to give to God."

My situation was illuminated. My normal was not a healthy normal, with the way each episode of Jack's anger caused me to physically and mentally decline. My heart had been filling with anxiety with each daunting day that I was with Jack, and it seemed as if there was no light at the end of the tunnel.

I felt a bit melancholy as I packed my bags because I wasn't sure of the next time I would see my mother. To cheer me up, we decided to end our weekend on a good note with a little bit of airport shopping, then we shed our tears and parted ways.

My stomach turned as I sat on the plane and thought about how I would have to face Jack without the support of family and friends around me. In my mind, I was all on my own.

I happened to look up a few rows ahead of me where one of the wisest conference speakers sat. A sense of comfort washed over me as I was reminded that God had a mission for me. I remembered that the Lord would give me courage to face Jack. He would prepare me for a new normal that was healthy and safe.

NINETEEN

BUILDING COLLAPSE OF ATTACHMENTS

I entered the baggage claim area at the Amarillo Airport and spotted Jack. He stood by the door with my luggage in hand and waved me in the direction of our vehicle. "Come on, the car is out this way."

His gestures proved that he was not happy to see me. My heart sank as I took a deep breath and walked in his direction.

When we arrived home, I greeted the kids, then wondered what Jack had been saying to them about me. No matter what conversations took place, I knew I would be safe if I stayed out of the way. Jack was used to my non-confrontational ways, but for me to stay out of range from his anger would be new to him. I hoped my strategy would help me ride out my time under his roof, until I graduated from cosmetology school.

When Jack came home from work each night, I ran to the bedroom and tried to read the books I bought at the conference. The side effects of my breakdown and of the abuse I had been enduring left me unable to comprehend the material but I tried anyway, with the hope that something would stick.

Jack checked on me frequently to see what I was up to. He'd stare at me for a few seconds then make a snide remark.

"I suppose you're reading those books from the conference so you can preach to me about how I should live my life!"

I shook my head. "No, Jack, everything I learned at the conference was for my ears only, not yours."

My answer agitated Jack, causing him to fume with anger.

Divided Home

Jack came home from work on a Thursday night and announced that he planned to sign up for credit card insurance, in case something happened to the card holder, which was me. We had been forced into bankruptcy shortly after buying the house, and when Jack was denied credit, he'd signed me up for a few credit cards. Now, I became concerned with his sudden desire to make sure that the cards would be paid off, as if he were preparing for something to happen to me.

Life with Jack was grim. I encouraged him to relax in the pool with us, but he showed no desire to participate.

"Jack, would you like to swim with us?"

"No!"

I quit asking him to join us after I had dreams about being drowned, rolled up in the pool cover, and carried off in a barrel by a semi truck.

A few days after Jack established the credit card insurance, he authorized the kids to have free time with video games. With a stance of defiance and a glare of intimidation, Jack slammed shut the sliding glass door that led to the pool. I then heard a loud rip emanate throughout the room as he quickly raced the drapes across the track. He was closing off any visibility or clear audibility that the kids might have from where they were inside to the pool outside.

I knew Jack well enough to know when he had a plan and when he was determined to complete it. With a serious look and thunder in his voice, he pointed me out and commanded, "Let's go swim!"

Jack's aggressive behavior from the last few months was still fresh in my mind. I sat at the kitchen table with no intention to move out of my chair, and continued to work on a project with Samantha. I looked up at Jack as I softly refused his offer with a simple shake of my head.

Jack pointed his finger and jolted toward me in anger as he hissed through his teeth. "I do not know what you are up to but I will get to the bottom of this!" He was referring to my refusal to bend to his every demand.

I knew Jack felt threatened by the renewed confidence I had gained from the women's conference but for me to tell him no, not only saved my life that day but it also exacerbated his anger.

A couple days later, I opened my email on the computer that Jack had fished back out of the dumpster after my rash act of rebellion. I started to write an email to tell my mom about Jack's aggression, but found myself scrolling through our past correspondences. The trail of letters dating back a few months, even from before the conference, reminded me of the misery I had endured and how necessary it was for me to follow through with my plans to take the kids and leave him. As I sat there reading, Jack surprised me by coming home earlier than usual. I abruptly stood up and left the computer desk. Before I realized what I had just given him access to, Jack took over the computer chair and began to scroll the document on the screen. He tightly pursed his lips together, then his eye began to twitch. I looked over at the computer screen and noticed that I had forgotten to close my email account. Jack jumped up with belligerence. His words hit my soul like a bullet as I felt the familiar fear that came with the start of another verbal attack. His eyes glazed over, his face filled with red splotches, and I watched his nostrils as they began to expand from the deep breaths he took in. Jack had read all the information I'd disclosed to my mother about the way he treated me, and he now knew about the secret runaway money.

"How dare you go behind my back and talk to your mother about the way I have treated you?" he yelled. "I thought I could trust you. I am the only one who is allowed to counsel any member of this family, and you should have never talked to her about me! There is nothing worse than discussing what goes on in this family with anybody other than me. You have betrayed me and you will pay for this!"

Sparks of Discernment

Accountability

Imagine a firefighter in the midst of a structure fire. Crawling along the floor in an attempt to stay under the thick black smoke, he reaches out around him to feel for the arm or leg of his accountability partner. Knowing he only has seven minutes remaining on his breathing apparatus, he fights panic. After separating from the rest of the search and rescue team, he realizes that they may have evacuated without him. With no visible access to the outside world, he knows he must act quickly, before the growing flames consume him. As he takes his ax to the wall to make a hole to crawl through, he hears the evacuation horns sound on the fire trucks outside, and he knows he is close to safety. With crackling flames three feet from his body, he pushes himself through the hole, barely escaping with his life.

When abuse flares up in your life, the last thing that you want is to be separated from loved ones who help to keep you accountable for your actions and help you to see that what you are going through is not acceptable. In the same way, your abuser must be held accountable for his or her actions, or the burning house (their damaging behavior) will collapse around them, in one way or another. There is a small chance that progress can be made without an accountability partner, but like the lone firefighter in the building being engulfed in flames, the risk is far too high.

Accountability is a necessity for safe living and it is a right that every human should exercise. Often when we are in danger, we tend to pull away from others, leaving us without an accountability partner.

In the Old Testament, even the kings weren't above seeking counsel from their advisers. "Plans fail for lack of counsel, but with many advisers they succeed." **(Proverbs 15:22 NIV).**

The spouse who says, "Nobody has the right to tell me what to do with my family," will not accept guidance or direction from an outside source. Unfortunately, he or she also demands all the members of the family to seek counsel and accountability from him or her alone. These methods allow the abuser to lead his or her family down a path of selfish gain. Eventually, the victims are left wounded with physical, emotional, and sometimes mental side effects. When this is the case, it is time to call upon your own search and rescue team (family, church members, counselor, doctor, or even police) to help you escape the burning home.

The Authoritarian

After Jack read the emails from my mom, he announced that we would begin to have family counsel time in the evenings after dinner in the family room.

During the first counsel session, before Jack began to speak, he pulled out a large flip pad of paper and set it on a handmade easel. He explained that he could treat us however he wished, and could sin in whatever fashion he desired without consequences, because God's grace rules over all sin. As he talked, he illustrated his points on the large paper, as if to clarify and drive the point home: his word was law here, even above God's.

I cringed as I thought about Jack's new theological beliefs. I was disappointed that he had chosen to serve his sinful nature over God's pure and righteous desires.

Jack had no evidence of humility left in him. His motives were impure and tainted with a satanic influence. I knew God would eventually show that He disapproved of Jack's actions.

Jack had learned to love unconditionally, which means to love others no matter how they treat you. He recently threw that philosophy out the window and only cared for people based on what they could do for him.

Jack would not extend grace to the kids or me for our mistakes, though he claimed and expected that grace for himself. He treated us as if we were robots without feelings, wishes, or dreams. We were expected to remain indifferent and emotionless to all his demands, and act perfectly in all our ways.

The second time Jack counseled us, he pranced with might and strength as he exalted himself. He then spoke awful words from his rotten heart.

"I never once want you to believe that you have the right to live with me in this house," he said. "All of you should feel privileged that I have allowed you to live here with me. As your father, I no longer need to put myself out for you emotionally. I only need to make sure you have food in your mouths and some type of clothes to wear to keep the police off my back, so they don't take you away from me. There is nowhere in the law that states that I, as your father, must make sure that you live in an emotionally stable environment."

Jack paused for a moment to take in and relish the rejected reactions from the faces of our children. He gloated with satisfaction at their shock. "Another thing," he continued. "You are old enough to live without your mother around. You no longer need her here for anything!"

Jack left the room, ending the conversation.

The look on the faces of my three children proved their fear of Jack. I was petrified and bewildered that his selfish behavior had mutated into a detestable hatred for the kids.

When we gathered for the third session, Jack talked to the kids as if they were slaves.

"I'm thinking about buying what I need to remodel this house," he informed them. "I'll purchase the supplies and have everything sitting outside. I will expect you kids to do the remodeling."

The hair on the back of my neck stood straight out.

"Now you wait a minute," I spoke with authority. "You know better than that. You need to find out how to remodel each project for yourself and be a part of the process. You can't order them around like robots and command them to fix this place with no direction!"

"Yes I can, and I will!" Jack spoke with no concern or compassion.

"How are they going to know how to fix it if nobody will guide them?" I fired back.

"They have the Internet!" he retorted. "They can look up the information they need and if they don't get it right, they will have to do it again."

I hid my eyes from this ugly beast that stood before me. He sought to rule over our home with power and control like a heartless king who expected us to bow before him and grovel for his mercy.

Sparks of Discernment

Conduction of Anger

In my situation, Jack's anger gained momentum without fuel from an outside source. I usually remained passive to avoid combustion.

But when the kids were the source of Jack's anger, the heat of his anger radiated onto me and my thermal conductivity went up, causing a fire of indignation to set things right for the kids. Unfortunately, the heat of my emotions created more thermal energy to convect heat in an upward motion which caused Jack to dig his heels in deeper over the subject, making the scenario worse for the kids.

The scenario is one that is too familiar for families dealing with emotional abuse. It's always good to stand up for your kids but it is never okay to make the situation worse for them. Safety always takes priority so as to lessen the effects of emotional trauma on their brains. Many times we forget that we have a way out of the situation when we are in the thick of an angry dispute and we forget that we can throw water on the emotional fire by calling a trusted friend, pastor, counselor, or in more severe cases, 911.

Weapon

I was tired of the way Jack demeaned my looks, my aptitude, and my personality. I didn't feel comfortable being in close proximity to him while I slept. I pulled my pillow off the bed, walked out to the family room, then grabbed a few blankets from the corner of the family room. I lay on the couch and snuggled up between the back of the couch and the seat cushions. My back ached and I struggled to get comfortable, so I stood up, then slid down to a spot on the floor. There was too much on my mind and I just couldn't sleep. I flipped over to lay on my back and realized that the night would only bring rest for my body but not for my mind.

Deep in the night, I heard a floorboard in the hallway creak just outside of Jack's room. There was a long pause and then another creak. I listened as the pattern continued, then I heard the knife drawer in the kitchen slowly and quietly being pulled open. There was a clank and then a ting. The air was quiet for a moment, until Jack's tall figure stood at the top of the two steps that went down into the family room.

Jack was unaware that I was awake. He whispered under his breath as he paced the length of the kitchen floor at the top of the two steps. After he paced the floor a few times he stopped and whispered under his breath, "I can't do it, I just can't do it."

The room grew quiet. I waited for him to walk in my direction but instead he paced the floor and whispered a little louder, "I need to, but I just can't do it."

I lay still and strategized my plan of escape in case he came toward me. I listened as Jack continued to argue with himself as he paced the floor, over and over again.

All of a sudden the room grew extremely quiet. I wasn't sure where he went. I peeked through squinted eyelids but could no longer see him. To my surprise, I heard Jack quietly slip the knife back into the drawer and walk back to his bedroom, in the same fashion he had come out.

The incident was surreal. I lay on the floor in denial, refusing to believe that Jack's intentions were to kill me.

The Sky is Falling

My graduation from cosmetology school was a few weeks away. I pressed forward and lived each day as if the knife incident had never happened.

Our Friday night tradition was to allow the kids to stay up as late as they desired if they had completed their schoolwork and chores for the week.

Jack went to bed early and commanded me to follow him, so the kids could have free rein over the house and refrigerator. I lay down on my side of the bed, and Jack quickly rolled away from me.

Peace was in the air and it gave me a chance to think about how Jack's emotionally abusive tactics had evolved into a series of calamitous events. My thoughts were abruptly interrupted when a loud crash came from the bathroom at the end of the hallway. I jolted into an upright position and held my breath while I waited for a scream.

My stomach turned into knots as I rose from the bed. "Jack, did you hear that?"

"It was nothing, lie back down," he replied.

I grabbed my robe and ran to see what had caused the noise. I opened the bathroom door and took in the devastation. The bathroom walls and ceiling had fallen in. The age of the house was revealed in the exposed wooden structure. I gasped from the dust in the air and covered my mouth. On the floor lay three feet of drywall and insulation. I looked down and noticed a hump on the toilet, under the mess. I was afraid it was one of the kids.

"Hey, is everybody in the family room?" I called out.

Josiah responded with a hearty yes, then Peter and Samantha chorused their answer together. Reassurance set in after I knew they were safe. My heart rejoiced with relief but my mind was in dismay.

I closed the bathroom door, unsure of how to clean up the mess. I walked around the house for a while to allow my nerves to settle down, then went back to bed.

I couldn't sleep. All I could focus on was how Jack reacted to the bathroom collapse. I came to the conclusion that he would be glad if he no longer had to provide for me and the kids.

Open Vent

Peter and Josiah cleaned up the bathroom rubble in the days to follow. One week later, Jack was inflicted with excruciating back pain. He lay in bed and moaned in misery as he rolled his body into a fetal position.

"Jack, is there anything I can get you?"

"No, just leave me alone!" he screamed.

As his pain increased, his irrational behavior escalated. I wanted to escape the hostile environment. However, I wasn't as heartless as he was, and I couldn't allow him to rot in bed.

On the second day of Jack's affliction, he woke up early in the morning and crawled into the bathroom to kneel before the white throne.

On the third day, he woke up and slid his body across the floor like a slug. He could hardly pull himself up to the commode. I knew it would be the day I would call for an ambulance.

I lay in bed and waited for Jack to ask for help, but he quieted himself and I fell back asleep. I suddenly woke with a sharp pain in my arm. I groaned as I tried to open my eyes. Confusion clouded my mind as I tried to figure out what had just hit me. I looked toward the bathroom with squinted eyes and realized that Jack had whipped the alarm clock at me from six feet away.

"Do you want help now?" I quietly asked in a groggy morning voice.

"No," Jack spat back at me with fury. "I'm in pain, and I don't think it is right for you to lie there and sleep while I slink around on the bathroom floor."

I knew God sought justice on behalf of the kids and me for how Jack treated us. I wished that he would give in and finally surrender his will to the Lord. However, I didn't want to deal with the tyrant in the bathroom for another day, so I called for an ambulance. Two Amarillo firefighters ran down from the fire station to assist the medic that was on duty.

I stayed in the front living room, out of range from Jack's wrath. When I had painted the room lavender, I had taken the cover off of the vent and had never put it back. As I stayed out of the way of Jack's medical help, I stared into the vent hole. Standing there, I was reminded of the closed heat vent in the guest room of Jack's parents when I'd first met them. I clearly recalled how Stella bellowed as she berated me and my family.

I recalled that in all the years past, I had kept the vent closed on the issues of mistreatment and disrespect from Jack and his family. But now I could see that the cover needed to be taken off so that our dysfunctions would be exposed and we could heal. I knew our friends and family would hear how Jack disregarded God's ways, how he was disrespectful and emotionally abusive toward the kids and me. We didn't deserve to live like that. Instead, we needed to feel respected, secure, and loved.

Amusement Park

Eventually Jack's pain dissipated and he recovered. Things started to get back to normal, or at least our version of it. The weather beckoned me to do something fun with the kids. Just then, Jack's parents called and invited us to join them at the finest amusement park in town.

The day turned out to be an adventure for Jack when he chose to ride the spinning cups twice in a row. On his second spin, I could see that he didn't feel well. Jack walked off the ride and into the restroom to work out his issues.

Thirty minutes later, we pulled Jack out of the restroom and placed him in a wheelchair. He was having severe muscle spasms that caused him to have no control over his body.

Stella grabbed the wheelchair and wheeled Jack out to the van, while the whole family trailed behind them. Before putting

Jack in the van, we allowed him to rest outside in the wheelchair for a while.

I stood in silence as I observed Jack's position. His eyes were wide open and his head was forced to look up at the sky. His tongue hung off to the side of his mouth, unable to utter a sound. Jack rested his elbows on the armrests of the wheelchair with his palms open and facing upward, toward the heavens.

Proud Jack had been immobilized and was forced into a position to praise God, if not through his heart then through his stance.

On this day, Jack was given a chance to give glory to God the Father, just as King Nebuchadnezzar was also given a chance, in the book of Daniel.

King Nebuchadnezzar walked in arrogance on the roof of his palace in Babylon and boasted, "I have built this great city as my royal home. I built it with my own power to show my glory and my majesty." **(Daniel 4:28-30 paraphrased)**.

Jack had misused his authority as the head of our home and also boasted of the home he built, just as Nebuchadnezzar did. He showcased his power and arrogance while he recklessly mistreated each family member.

"The words were still in his mouth when a voice from heaven said, 'These things will happen to you; your royal power has been taken away from you. You will be forced away from people. You will live with the wild animals in the field and will be fed on grass like an ox. Seven years will pass before you learn this lesson: the Most High God rules over every kingdom on earth and gives those kingdoms to anyone He chooses.' Immediately the words came true.

Nebuchadnezzar was forced away from the people and he began eating grass like an ox. He became wet from dew. His hair grew long like the feathers of an eagle, and his nails grew like the claws of a bird. At the end of that time, I, Nebuchadnezzar, looked up toward heaven, and I could think normally again! Then I gave praise to the Most High God." **(Daniel 4:31-34a).**

I waited for Jack to heal from being immobilized and wondered if he, too, would choose to serve God, or if he would continue to seek the wicked desires of his heart.

TWENTY

FIREFIGHTER DOWN

Stella nursed Jack back to health just in time for my graduation ceremony in October of 2007. After the ceremony, we went out for dinner with Stella and Wayne. Jack acted as if he had no animosity toward me, and proved he could be kind and full of compassion. His gentleness and love confused me.

The next evening after Jack came home from work, he asked, "When are you going to get a job?"

"I have been overloaded on stress and I need to take a few weeks to recover before I apply for work," I replied.

Jack rolled his eyes and showed his disapproval.

"Fine!" He grabbed his keys to the car and stormed out the front door.

Now that graduation was over and we were out of the public eye, Jack reverted back to his hateful ways. In my heart, I wanted to get up and leave but all my strength had been zapped from me. I felt as if my body had given up on life, against my will.

As each day passed, I slipped a little deeper into depression and began to shut down emotionally. I couldn't cry or sleep, and I couldn't hold a conversation with anybody for more than a few minutes. My thoughts had become disoriented and I realized I'd had an unrealistic view of my life with Jack. I was finally realizing that there would never be an amicable solution that would allow us to continue on a path together. There was no end game in which we would both be happy. For many years, I had lied to myself and thought that things would get better. I knew the truth now. I lived in a house of mirrors with a madman. I listened to him as he beat me down with his abusive words and watched as he poured his spiteful ways on me.

I felt like a sea sponge that had been taken out of its natural environment where it had once been loved and nourished. I, like the sponge, had soaked up all the oxygen-rich nutrients that surrounded me, which included the time and love others invested in me. Now it seemed as if Jack had wrung all that out of me.

My life was now brittle and dry, like a sea sponge becomes after it is pulled from the water. I had nothing left to give. I felt as if Jack had thrown me to the floor and stomped on me with his hateful actions, shattering my spirit into a thousand pieces.

Every night, I had a recurring dream that appeared in black and white. The dream became more vivid as each night passed, and in it, it seemed as if my life was about to come to an end.

In the dream, my spirit sat on the top of a train that was headed for a low-clearance tunnel made of brick. Just before the train car entered the tunnel, I woke up. I no longer woke with a jerking motion and a gasp of fear, like one does when they feel as if they are falling off a cliff. But it became increasingly clear to me, as I reflected on my dream in my waking moments, that my spirit was going to die if I did not get out of my current situation. I needed to get off of this train.

In the days to follow, Jack tried to motivate me out of my state of despondency. He yelled at me with overtones of condemnation. He approached me as if I were a child who needed direction and discipline, and used my broken state of mind to begin a new round of emotional beatings. Each round started at four o'clock in the morning with the sound of the alarm, one hour before he had to get ready for work.

I could hear Jack down the hallway. He quietly shut Samantha's bedroom door first, then made his way to the boys' room to close their door. Jack then quickened his pace as he arrogantly made his way over to me in his robe of righteousness. I laid lifelessly on the couch as he hunched over me, one foot from my face, and began his merciless rage of mind-wrecking words.

Jack's one hour rant put me in a trance and caused me to be effortlessly captured in his evil spell. I experienced his curse and watched him transform into the beast of Leviathan.

Jack's voice deepened with anger when he spoke his words of hate. He hissed, enunciating each word between his teeth with a spray of venomous saliva. "You are *not* needed here anymore. We do *not* need you in this family! Those kids do *not* need you as a mother anymore!"

The beast of Leviathan had unleashed his great might and strength over my weak and powerless body.

A Detailed Description of Leviathan:

"No one is brave enough to make it angry, I will speak about Leviathan's arms and legs, its great strength, and well-formed body. No one can tear off its outer hide or poke through its double armor. No one can force open its great jaws; they are filled with frightening teeth. It has rows of shields on its back that are tightly sealed together. When it snorts, flashes of light are thrown out, and its eyes look like the light at dawn. Flames blaze from its mouth; sparks of fire shoot out. Smoke pours out of its nose, as if coming from a large pot over a hot fire. Its breath sets coals on fire, and flames come out of its mouth. There is great strength in its neck. People are afraid and run away. The powerful people fear its terrible looks and draw back in fear as it moves. The sword that hits it does not hurt it, nor the arrows, darts and spears. It treats iron as if it were straw and bronze metal as if it were rotten wood. Clubs feel like pieces of straw to it, and it laughs when they shake a spear at it." **(Job 41:10-29)**.

I had two goals each day: to keep breathing, and not become Leviathan's pitiful snack.

TWENTY ONE

COMPLICATED EGRESS

"*B*ut there may be an angel to speak for him, one out of a thousand, who will tell him what to do. The angel will beg for mercy and say: 'Save him from death. I have found a way to pay for his life.' " **(Job 33:23-24).**

I put a barricade up around my heart to preserve my spirit when I realized that I could no longer be the wife who doted on Jack while he treated me abusively.

I stood up and slowly moved my feeble body through the house to the bathroom. I turned the faucet on and filled the tub with warm water, then added some sea salt.

Though the boys and I had cleaned up the mess after the initial disaster in the bathroom, nothing had been done to actually fix the damage. The air in the small, demolished room was cold but I didn't care. I was behind a locked door, away from Jack's cruelty. With a sad heart, I looked around the barren bathroom walls. All that was visible was the wooden framing. I could see how the room was sectioned off from the other rooms that surrounded it. There was no evidence that the drywall and insulation had ever existed. We were poor, not only financially but spiritually.

The wooden framing reminded me of what we are like without Christ in our lives. We have the frame of our bodies to hold us up, and we are able to function within it. But without Christ we are barren and empty inside, and it eventually leaves us hopeless and vulnerable.

My thoughts were interrupted by a knock on the bathroom door. It was Peter. I could tell he was concerned about me as he spoke.

"Mom, Dad bought us ice cream," he said. "Do you want to come out and join us?"

I was sad that I had allowed my kids to endure this trial of abusive nonsense and I felt guilty that I had to turn my son's invitation down. I gently answered him, "No, thank you."

I heard a disappointed sigh, and knew my answer was heard.

I finished my bath and gingerly walked out to the living room. Jack and the kids held their empty containers of ice cream and abruptly finished their conversation.

The kids briefly looked up at me with disturbed looks. I could see the invisible tears by the expressions left on their faces. The thought quickly ran through my mind, *I don't know how to end this abuse, I don't know which step to take next.*

Everybody quietly left the family room with their eyes cast to the floor. Not a word was spoken as they headed off to bed. I was left alone in the quietness of the cold, dark room to pray.

As I drifted off to sleep that night, I thought about how physically, mentally, and spiritually broken I had become. I'd had the wrong idea of what a submissive wife was, and had fallen into a trap of twisted lies that took away my freedom, rights, independence, and identity. I had been trained to not question my husband's motives and had learned to stay neutral on all issues with him, in order to avoid his tactics of intimidation.

I now knew that God did not intend for submission to be misused against me, and I understood that the Lord was on a mission to rescue me. There is a story in Acts Chapter 12 (verses 7-9a) in which King Herod had chained Saint Peter up in prison.

"Suddenly, an angel of the Lord stood there, and a light shined in the cell. The angel struck Peter on the side and woke him up. 'Hurry! Get up!' the angel said. And the chains fell off Peter's hands. Then the angel told him, 'Get dressed and put on your sandals.' And Peter did. Then the angel said, 'Put on your coat and follow me.' So Peter followed him out."

Having been active in the church my whole life, and an avid reader of the Bible, I was familiar with these step-by-step instructions that Saint Peter followed to freedom. But I never dreamed that I would know firsthand how that would feel.

Jack showed up again at four o'clock in the morning, just as he had done every day for the last two weeks.

I looked down and noticed that I was in the same position as when I'd fallen asleep. I then looked up at Leviathan as he tore out my soul with a premeditated verbal assault for the next hour. Jack made it clear to me that I was not beautiful, inside or out, and that I had no redeemable value. I was rubbish. He finished his rant with his all-too-familiar last words:

"You are *not* needed here anymore. We do *not* need you in this family! Those kids do *not* need you as a mother anymore!"

Then he swiftly left the room with an air of righteousness.

I sat up and became filled with fear. Something was different. It seemed that he'd left the room more quickly than usual. He acted as if he had a new plan this time, and I was afraid he would come back to end my life.

I felt as if the Holy Spirit Himself welled up inside me and renewed my strength. I then heard Him speak. "Go now, just leave quietly."

I wanted to take the kids with me, like I promised, but I knew Jack would stop me in my tracks and feared what he might do to me.

I grabbed my purse off the chair where I had placed it the night before. *Where's my cell phone? I have got to look for my cell phone.*

It was then that I heard the Holy Spirit. It's in your purse, leave now. My heart raced as I anxiously opened the screen door of the house and held it to avoid a loud slam.

Nervously, I slipped out into the dark morning. I held my breath and frequently checked behind me, to be sure Jack hadn't followed me outside.

Skittishly, I walked over to the car and glanced up one last time before I opened the door to get in. In fear, I held the door open and carefully drove off, then slammed it shut after I was a safe distance from Jack.

Suddenly, I felt as if the Lord had breathed life into me and my mind had fallen out of the trance it had been in for so long. I began to think about what I needed to do next. *I will come back and get the kids with the police, after I file a police report. I will be safe with that plan and Jack will not be able to hurt us anymore.*

My heart beat with exuberance as I drove onto the expressway. I briefly looked up at the sky and watched the beautiful stars dance upon the black canvas.

God was with me. I felt His presence and an insurmountable peace overtook my soul. I was not afraid!

Then the Holy Spirit reminded me of **Genesis 15:5-6**.

"Then God led Abram outside and said, 'Look at the sky. There are so many stars you cannot count them. Your descendants also will be too many to count.' Abram believed the Lord. And the Lord accepted Abram's faith, and that faith made him right with God."

I knew at that point, I too had made my heart right with God. My faith in Him had been restored because I obeyed the Lord and finally left Jack.

TWENTY TWO

FIREWALL OF PROTECTION FOR VICTIMS

I watched the morning sun appear as I drove around to look for the police station. I could see it in my head, but I could not remember which street it was on.

I called my friend Sarah. There was no answer. I stopped at a nearby grocery store to pick up a few items that the kids and I would need. I spent exactly one hundred dollars on survival food to match the hundred dollars Jack had spent on himself when he was offended by the letters we wrote to him in Grawn.

I returned to my car and tried to call Sarah again. She answered this time, and met me at the grocery store a few minutes later. I followed her to the police station and we went in together.

I began to tell my story to the officer and I watched his face as it filled with disappointment.

"Ma'am, do you want to file a police report?"

Sarah spoke up before I could reply. "Yes, she does," she said.

I sat quietly, thankful that Sarah was with me. I had never been inside a police station before and I was intimidated by the process I had to go through.

"What is it that you need to report?"

"Jack has been emotionally abusive," I answered.

My eyes shifted in shame as I wondered if I could report something like that. The words sounded foolish when they came out of my mouth and I felt stupid.

The officer furrowed his brow. "I'm sorry, ma'am, I need more specifics than that. Has he broken the law in any other way?"

"Well, over a month ago he stood at the top of the steps in the family room with a knife in his hand and quietly began to argue with himself, 'I can't do it, I just can't do it.' Then he paused and said, 'I have to do it, I just have to.' He eventually talked himself out of it and went back to bed."

"Do you have a date and time as to when that incident happened?"

"I know it was in September, and it was early in the morning, sometime after one."

"I need the date and time it happened, otherwise I cannot process a report."

I slumped down in my chair as I tried to remember the exact date and time that Jack had attempted to kill me, but the trauma I experienced disrupted my memory. Disappointed in myself, I hung my head in shame because I could not recall the information I needed. Instead I looked at the police officer with a blank stare.

"Is there another event that has happened in the past that you can remember?"

"About six years into our marriage, Jack admitted that he hired a hitman for two hundred dollars to kill me and the kids," I said.

"Did you file a report with this information?"

"No."

I sat quietly, thinking about all the misguided advice that I'd received from church officials. I remembered that I was told not to involve the police or file a report about Jack's plan to kill us. I now knew that the advice they gave me was wrong, and realized how valuable that police report could've been in helping my current situation.

The officer frowned. "Unfortunately, without the information we need and without the previous report, we can't do anything about your situation." He paused for a moment, then continued. "I'm sorry to tell you, too much time has lapsed since the incident of the planned drive-by shooting to file an updated report. Unfortunately, there is nothing I can do for you."

"Can I file a restraining order against Jack?" I asked, exasperated. I was getting nowhere.

The police officer gave a compassionate look and a soft nod as he turned away from me to get the information I needed.

Sarah and I walked over to another building to file the restraining order, but my request was denied because I was unable to recall the necessary information to file the police report.

I was scared. I wasn't sure if Jack would hire another hitman, or perhaps take my life with his own hands.

I tried to put my fears behind me as we walked to the Human Services building to talk to a counselor. The counselor was kind and knowledgeable. I felt safe and at ease around her. I opened up and told her how Jack had treated me and that he had sexually assaulted me.

"Did you tell him no?" she asked.

"I was in shock and scared that he would cause more physical harm if I told him no," I spoke out of frustration.

The counselor frowned and then explained, "When you are filing a report, no charges can be pressed unless you told the perpetrator no."

She then handed me a sheet of paper titled, *Power and Control*. I read the list that identified abusive characteristics. To my surprise, I was able to place a checkmark next to each and every abusive characteristic listed. I now had confirmation, to prove to myself that I was a victim of abuse, even though Jack had never physically beaten me.

I quickly accepted my reality, then asked the counselor if they could hide my family from Jack. But because I failed to file police reports in years past, and there were no signs of physical violence, nothing could be done to help me.

Sparks of Discernment

Validating Emotional Abuse Trauma

When I left the police station after I filed my report, I felt stupid. I felt as if my report sounded like I was in the third grade complaining about how little Bobby threw stones at me while he screamed inappropriate language. We must not minimize our experience of emotional abuse based on the inability to press charges for the way we are being treated. Likewise, do not be discouraged by the reaction of the officer taking your report, if he or she does not seem to legitimize your distress. There may not be any charges you can file against the perpetrator, but you can certainly file a report to create that paper trail. This helps to show a pattern of your abuser's aggressive behavior and to build a case against them, to protect you. Though it can be difficult to have the presence of mind to do so when you are being attacked (verbally or physically), take note of the date and time, and report whether or not there were any witnesses.

California recognizes emotional abuse as domestic abuse if your psychiatrist writes up a report that confirms the distress. Familiarize yourself with the laws in your state and how they apply to emotional abuse. In some states, if a counselor documents the emotional abuse and orders an emergency protective order for the victim, a restraining order against the aggressor will be issued. If you have a witness who will talk about the maltreatment at the time it occurs, that is in your favor. Call the police when you are unsure of what your abuser is going to do next and his or her actions indicate irrational, explosive behavior. But understand that if you report it, you must be prepared for the police to arrest the abuser if they find legal reason to do so. It is also important to examine the fact that if you have had to call the police on your significant other, things are *not* going to get better. It is time to get out of that situation for good.

Typically, one does not go to jail for emotional abuse because it is not a criminal offense. Each situation must be evaluated on a case-by-case basis. Keep in mind that there are many other factors that are considered when a report is being made that you may not be aware of and that can favor the victim. That is why it is so important to allow the police to question you in person and to see the premises where the emotional abuse took place.

At first, your validation must come from what you know is the truth. But to just report it to the police is not enough. It's important that you see a counselor. Having your experience validated will help you with your healing process. If you do not get counseling, you may minimize the experience over time in your mind. We are in dire need of law reform concerning various degrees of assault and domestic violence, and often the process of reporting the offenses to seek safety and justice can be just as scary as the abuse itself. Find a support system as you fight this uphill battle. You are not alone.

Please be serious about doing what is best for you. You need to take care of yourself and be safe. Your trauma is real, your feelings are valid, and you have the right to a safe space to heal.

Psychiatric Ward

Next, I found myself inside the psychiatric ward, ready to report Jack's behavior. The woman at the front desk listened to my story then said, "You can report him, but if we bring him in and the test proves to be negative, then you will be fined fifteen hundred dollars."

I stepped back to think about my decision. *Am I positive that*

Jack is psychotic? Or is his behavior something he has control over? Did he treat everybody else the way he treated me?

I made my decision based on three factors. The first factor was based on Stella's warning about Jack being a compulsive liar. The second factor was based on what Jack had told me himself: "I have learned to control how my body will respond when I lie," he'd said. "And I know I could pass a lie detector test if I took one."

With Jack being a good liar, I was afraid he would probably answer the test questions to favor his release without being treated for his condition. The third factor was based on how Jack acted. I saw his abusive tendencies to be both conscious and subconscious. Subconsciously, he would react to certain scenarios based on learned behavior. I was inclined to think that the last two years with Jack were more conscious, meaning that he intentionally tried to push me out of the family.

I was scared, and felt that I didn't have enough information to prove that Jack was insane. Based on my fears, I chose to walk away and not report his behavior to the psychiatric ward.

Back at the Homestead

Sarah asked the police to meet us at my house later that morning. I wanted to go back home to pick up the kids and a few of our belongings.

When we arrived, I found Samantha locked in the van with Stella and Wayne. They were ready to drive away, but Sarah blocked them in when she pulled up behind them. I tried to coax Samantha out of the van, but the messages she received from Stella and Wayne confused her.

"Don't look up," I heard Stella say to my daughter. "Keep your head down. Samantha, Samantha, don't look up."

All I wanted was a chance to speak to my child and allow her to voice her opinion, but we were both denied that right.

I walked over to the front lawn where Jack had our boys lined up in military formation. Their eyes spoke to Jack with worry and pain as they glanced many times in his direction.

"Peter," I said. "I came back for you, do you still want to come with me?"

Peter fearfully glanced at his father as he stepped forward and answered with insecurity, "No, ma'am."

He stepped back in line, and then Josiah stepped forward.

"Josiah, I came back for you, do you still want to come with me?" I asked.

Josiah, with the same rehearsed facial expressions as Peter, answered, "No, ma'am."

I stood back for a moment and observed the scene. My boys were acting skittish and fearful, as if they would get hit in the head or punished later for not doing the "right" thing.

I had stood between Jack and the boys on many occasions, but now I was worried. I would no longer be able to act as their buffer, to protect and defend them from their dad's emotional abuse. I wondered, *Do they understand the full impact of their decision?*

The last time I'd discussed the abuse with the boys, they had begged me not to leave them behind.

I swallowed my fear for my children, gathered the five shirts and two pairs of pants I owned, along with my cosmetology supplies and my lavender plant, and walked away from Jack's abuse without my babies.

When I walked out the front door, I thought to myself, *They made a choice to stay with Jack and I need to let them see for themselves what he is like.*

The following Sunday I woke up with the freedom to go to church without any repercussions from Jack. I called my three kids on the phone and invited them to come with me. As I got ready to go, I glanced at my lavender plant and smiled. *What a journey we have been on!* This little plant had been my companion, and though at times I had been confused about its purpose, it seemed so clear now. A little research had uncovered the fact that many people view lavender as a symbol of new beginnings and healing. My current situation was messy, but I had successfully branched off onto a new path.

My emotions were a roller coaster, and from riding the high of my new freedom, I plummeted along with the sinking feeling in my stomach when I thought of my children, who were not yet free. The familiar anxiety grew as I drove back to Jack's domain. I was stunned when I pulled up to the front of the house to pick the kids up for church. Jack's girlfriend had parked her car in the driveway. The morning dew that covered her windows told me everything I needed to know.

As I drove off with the kids, I felt my roller coaster climb again. I rejoiced in my heart that God had provided a replacement for me, just as He had provided a replacement for Isaac on Mount Moriah, when Abraham built an altar before the Lord. **(Genesis 22).**

My anxious spirit left me when I realized that I had indeed been set free from Jack's abusive grip. I was confident that Jack would not pursue me, since he already had a new love interest.

Hidden

Sarah was kind enough to let me hide myself at her home for six weeks. The peaceful environment allowed me to sleep, something I hadn't done in a long time.

The shock from the emotional trauma flooded my mind and caused fatigue. My heart broke and I mourned, as Jack was no longer allowing me to see the kids.

One afternoon, a tall man stood at Sarah's door. He handed me a document that said I was being sued. Jack wanted a divorce and expected to get everything. I didn't want to fight. I just wanted my kids, the camping gear, and the homeschool books.

My restless spirit knew that Jack's next step would be made soon. He sought revenge and I knew that I would eventually pay, just like he promised. He still wanted to control me, if not physically, then he would do it mentally. I knew he would eventually move far away, to make it impossible for me to visit my kids.

One month after I left, in December of 2007, Jack called me on the phone and asked if I was ready to come home. I hesitated before speaking, as I tried to catch my breath.

"Jack, you made your choice when you allowed your girlfriend to move in."

I couldn't believe that he thought that I would be willing to come back to him after everything he put me through. I was broken, and I knew it would take years to recover from the abuse he put me through.

TWENTY THREE

RESTORATION FROM DESTRUCTION

he firehouse radio crackled as a call for a large structure fire was dispatched in. As I rushed to jump into my gear, memories of my past haunted my mind. Why did I allow Jack's abusive influence to rule my life? And why did I have such a hard time forgiving myself for staying under his tyranny?

I had fought off the demons of sorrow for many years and knew that a fire call was the only thing that broke the cycle of sadness from my abusive past. Samantha had graduated a year before and my boys were still out of contact with me. I knew I could avoid the grief of loneliness if I kept busy at the firehouse. The Lord gave me the desire to become a firefighter. Serving the community in this manner satisfied what I missed at my apartment, where I was living alone for the first time in a long time. For years, Jack had isolated me from my loved ones, and did his best to turn my family against me. It was taking time for me to regain the confidence in myself that I did, indeed, have a place amongst those who never stopped loving me and caring for me. It was a process, and sometimes being alone at my apartment made it difficult to fight the thoughts and bad energy that had been ingrained in me throughout all those years of abuse with Jack.

My fire crew descended on the truck that was already running and ready to go. I wanted the front seat, but my fire brother beat me to it when he called, "Shotgun!" The truth was, it didn't matter where any of us sat. We would head toward the danger together. We had each other's backs, a feeling that had been so foreign to me during my years of isolation. Here at the firehouse, I had a family. Here, we held each other up in good times and bad.

As we headed out to the fire, our fire truck slid sideways over the ice-covered road. I loved the adventure and risk that my job brought, and lacked the fear another person might experience in the same situation. However, I had the necessary discretion that was needed to keep me from danger.

I instinctively sent up a quick prayer.

"Woo!" I hollered, trying to lighten up any tension that the dangerous roads brought on. The truck straightened itself out. Once we arrived at our destination, the colossal blaze took center stage. I was enraptured with the crackling sound of wood burning and bricks popping, while officers in charge commanded firefighters where to go.

I was caught up in my trance as I gazed at the fire. Then I heard the Lord, "Are you afraid?"

I shook my head no. Again, I heard His voice. "You are still scared of your abuser? You fear him, yet you dare to stand here in the midst of this three-story fire, ready to fight it without hesitation?"

The Lord was right, I knew I had the skill and courage to fight a fire that could swallow me whole, yet I still feared Jack. It was then that I knew I needed to finish what I had started when I'd silently escaped in the night years before. When I arrived home that evening, I picked up my pencil. I would write my story. I would face my past and conquer my fears. It was time to share my story of emotional abuse so that others could also recognize the signs and be set free.

Healing

Jack married thirty days after our divorce was final. My biggest fear came true. He packed up and moved the kids five states away from me.

Three years later, I received a phone call from Samantha. "Mom, I'm depressed and I don't want to live this way."

I took in a deep breath, then slowly let it out. "Samantha, let me talk to your dad so I can convince him that you should come live with me."

"No, mom, no!" Samantha pleaded. "Don't do that. He won't give you what you want."

I settled her fears and reassured her that she would be rescued. Samantha beat me to the task of approaching Jack with her desire to live with me. Jack responded with rejection, then seemed to waffle on the issue, as if contemplating how best to flex his control. Very quickly after his initial denial of Samantha's request, he called my mother and commanded her to pick Samantha up that night.

My mother lived too far away to obey Jack's instructions, but offered to pick up Samantha three days later.

After a few weeks had passed, I flew into Michigan from Texas. My heart broke as I held my skittish daughter. Her heart was damaged and her trust had been shattered by her father and stepmother. She had been rejected, neglected, and emotionally abused. Her body showed signs of malnourishment. She also suffered from an ulcer and needed two root canals.

My sweet baby girl had a tough exterior and a broken interior. My goal was to love and nurture her. I wanted to provide a stable environment where she would recover and have the freedom to express her emotions and creativity, just as every human should have the right to do. Over time, we grew together and moved forward on our paths toward healing. Eventually I was able to reunite with my sons as well, and as I have witnessed all of my children journey toward renewal and restoration, the pieces of my heart have begun to fit back together.

Redeemed

"Then his body is made new like a child's. It will return to the way it was when he was young. That person will pray to God, God will listen to him. He will see God's face and will shout with happiness. And God will set things right for him again." **(Job 33:25-26).**

In **1 Samuel 16-26** we read the story on how King David was King Saul's Armour Bearer. While David was under King Saul's rule, he learned how to prepare and train for battle. We as survivors of abuse must also prepare and learn to protect ourselves from our abusers.

One practical way to accomplish this is to sharpen the blade of our sword, the Word of God. We need to learn it and keep it ready for use in prayer, to battle the spiritual war we face. The Bible says,

"For our struggle is not against flesh and blood, but against the rulers, against the authorities, against the powers of this dark world and against the spiritual forces of evil in the heavenly realms." **(Ephesians 6:12 NIV).**

Before David became Saul's armour-bearer, he was called to play his harp for King Saul. David's music soothed the king from the evil spirit that influenced him, for he was tormented by the spirit and it caused him to be mentally unstable. When the music played, the evil spirit left.

Many abusers also struggle with an influence that causes them to be mentally unstable such as alcohol, drugs, or personality disorders. Victims of abuse get sucked into the dilemma and try to soothe the effect the influence has on their abuser, usually to the downfall and destruction of both the abuser and victim.

King Saul favored David because of the peace it brought to his life, until David killed Goliath with a stone from his sling. David's achievements won the hearts of many and King Saul became jealous, as he felt disquieted that the anointed King David would take the throne before his time. King Saul convinced himself that David was guilty of tyranny and pursued him for years to have him killed.

Many of us can relate to David's story. We are wooed into a relationship with someone who promises to protect and love us but for whatever reason-- always due to that person's own issues that are often projected onto others-- the justifications for abuse begin. That person develops a disdain toward you, then pursues the destruction of your character or the annihilation of your life. But we can be encouraged and allow our hope to rise just as it did for David. Fortunately, God led David to safety while he was on the run from the king, just as He continues to keep me safe from Jack, in spite of his threats from the past and any desire to kill me.

I stand amazed at the mighty ways the Lord has provided for me throughout my process of healing and how He has restored my relationships with my children. I missed out on a number of years, but through the tears of what I can't recover is the joy of discovery. It has been twelve years in the making and I am grateful that they can find it within themselves to forgive me for not being a better protector.

I would never wish for anyone else to suffer the trials and adversities that I did. The road of healing has been long and grueling. I have had to work hard to restore my health and my relationships with my children.

I never wanted my children to suffer as I did. I worked to protect them from the effects of emotional abuse, but they were impossible to escape. A parent can't hide abuse from the kids because the kids live it and see it, right along with the parent. If you have to ask yourself questions like, "Is this normal?" or "Is this abusive?" chances are, it isn't normal and yes, it is abusive. A doctor or counselor is the best place to start asking questions. Either of them can direct you to safe answers.

With pain comes healing. Many of us have heard the phrase, "What doesn't kill you makes you stronger." I would never want you to believe that I am stronger in the sense that I would be strong enough to go through an abusive experience again. I am strong now, only because I create boundaries to keep abusive influences out of my life.

My priorities have changed since the time that I lived under my abuser's oppression. I used to put the needs of my abuser before mine to create less conflict. In turn, I hurt my physical, mental, and spiritual well-being by not taking care of myself first.

I've learned that balance is essential in a relationship. Without balance, something or someone suffers. I suffered from PTSD, memory loss, low blood sugar, anemia, food allergies, digestive issues, and more, all because I lived in an emotionally abusive environment.

I now have a renewed strength that I have acquired through God's Word and the experiences He has given me to grow. One of those experiences was the realization of a dream that began as a mere seed of an idea-- becoming a firefighter. That experience has helped me gain dignity, courage, self-esteem, and confidence. Today, I can stand tall with a renewed spirit, knowing that the power of a flame is stronger and more destructive than my abuser. If I can fearlessly face a burning building that is engulfed in flames, then I can muster up enough courage to defend myself from my abuser.

You don't have to be able to put out a raging fire to know that you have the strength to overcome the abuse you have endured. Everyone has their own version of strength, perseverance, and methods for recognizing their ability to stand back up. You have your own version of a firefighter within that is waiting to remind you just what you are capable of.

There may not be much I can do now about any malicious intentions Jack might have toward me, but like the Biblical character King David, I must surround myself with an army and be familiar with the skills needed to protect myself, preparing for an attack if it were to ever manifest.

It frees me to know that I have the power to protect myself from Jack, so that I will never be the murder victim marked off with bright, yellow "DO NOT CROSS" tape. I continue to heal, and I extend waiting arms to those of you who will join me. Now is my time to celebrate my triumph. Though my spirit was pummeled, I now stand in the middle of the ring with my fist held high, indicating that I have overcome. Now is my time to breathe.

The scent of lavender accompanies the pure, life-giving oxygen that enters my lungs and lets me know I am moving forward on the right path. Now is my time to sing. I have found my song again, and it will never again get trapped in a cage of oppressing silence. Now is my time to lead. I have walked through the worst of my fire and emerged from the other side, not unscathed, but strong and determined. We will no longer simply survive. Now is our time to live.

Epilogue

When I first began attending cosmetology school, the course started with an extra credit challenge that would result in the winner receiving a free set of acrylics. I always wanted a set of nails, but it was a luxury I thought I would never experience. I worked hard to win the challenge and succeeded. After my instructor applied my hard-earned reward onto my fingers, I would sit at home and stare at my hands in my quiet moments. They looked beautiful, and I felt pampered and special. I felt beautiful, a feeling that had been missing for years, as Jack had served as a distorted mirror that spit an awful, ugly image of myself back at me.

In my last few weeks of cosmetology school I had

to build a portfolio and explain how I would use my education. I wrote a segment on how I would give back to my community by helping women who were less fortunate. I wanted them to feel important and special, just as I had when I received my reward at a time when I didn't have much. As my schooling wrapped up, I didn't quite know what it would look like for me to give back. What I found in the years to follow was that I had several interests and talents that could be combined to help others.

When I left Jack shortly after I graduated from school, I spent the next few years figuring out how to live on my own in a peaceful environment. As I grew back into the person I was always meant to be, I began to meet other women who also suffered from the effects of emotional abuse. God then gave me a desire to help them overcome those effects. It was throughout my cosmetology career that I realized I could very directly apply what I had felt when I won the contest in school. By lending a listening ear and a supportive shoulder to lean on while simply giving a victim a long-lasting shellac manicure, I was sending her a message. I was reminding her that she was worthy, had value, and was deserving of special treatment. In the weeks to follow, when she would look at her hands, each woman would see beauty, just as I had, and remember the encouraging words that were shared with her.

Once I moved back to Michigan, God gave me

direction regarding the path He set out for me. It was at this moment that I realized I had been issued a new set of freedom wings to share with others. But before I could fully dedicate my efforts to helping anyone else, I had to gain confidence in myself. Along my journey of healing, and after the initial seeds had been planted in my mind when I lived in Texas, I became a firefighter and learned to believe in myself. I found out that with knowledge, skill, and dedication, one could achieve what he or she sets out to do. Slowly but surely, self-confidence began to take shape, and all fear was squashed. Courage was achieved. Because of my training as a firefighter, I am now able to share how one can rise above her or his victimization and become a survivor with the courage and strength to fight for individual freedoms, experience joy, and find a new purpose in life.

I found that many women have twisted convictions that have been ingrained in them. Because of this, I went back to school to obtain a Bachelor's degree in Theology so that I could help others untwist the scriptures that were once used to cause adversity through manipulation, power, and control.

God has brought all of my experiences together to culminate in the start of a new ministry and a new vision. I started Under Abusive Influences Ministry (UAIM) to help women identify and recover from emotional abuse. As a Christian counselor, I strive to serve the oppressed in my community through UAIM. UAIM is where we aim for recovery from emotional abuse to gain our own sets of freedom wings.

Faith Under Fire Through Trials of Abuse was written to fulfill part of my purpose by sharing my story to unveil the truths of emotional abuse. My vision is to see recovery centers opened up for victims of emotional abuse because there is currently no real help for those who were not physically battered. Of the many things I encountered in my recovery, a safe and secure space dedicated solely to my healing was something that was noticeably lacking. Emotional abuse is just as real and damaging as physical abuse. There should be a haven awaiting anyone who seeks safety and recovery.

The healing process is continuous and evolving. It is difficult, but so worth digging in and doing. The process is different for everyone, but for everyone it involves a great deal of self-examination, not only of your current situation, but of the moments of impact throughout your life that led you to where you are now. At the time of publication of *Faith Under Fire Through Trials of Abuse*, I am working on completing a partner text, *When Ashes Bloom*. This guide will help readers delve more deeply into past trauma, triggers, and moments that shaped them. Dealing with the heartache that abuse brings, it will walk victims through a path of recovery that will help create a healthier environment for emotional healing. Churches and communities are also welcome to use the second book as a guide to help them form recovery centers.

Just as a forest fire burns the old to allow the new to sprout up, your emergence from the flames of your trials will allow for fresh growth in your life.

Activities and Resources For Recovery

1. Advice for Partners

GOD'S BROKEN FLOWERS

Women can be like flowers. For us to survive and thrive, we need our spouses to look out for us, not harm us. Our spouses need to provide the healthy soil that will nourish us and promote a healthy well-being.

If a man controls the flower and keeps her hidden away from the world, he has become selfish.

One of Adam's jobs was to tend the garden. Men, your garden is your wife. Give her a balanced life of love, affection, sun, water, nutrition, rest, and relaxation and she will thrive. Push her beyond her limits with unreasonable expectations and she will wither.

Sparks of Discernment

Isolation

"So brothers and sisters, be careful that none of you has an evil, unbelieving heart that will turn you away from the living God. But encourage each other every day while it is today." (Hebrews 3:12-13).

Living under abuse can cause you and your children to fall away from the Lord. The abuser's influence is stronger than you think. Their abusive behavior isolates members of the family by limiting or not allowing the victims to fellowship with other believers in Christ.

Isolation is a common tactic that abusers use to control their victims. It also includes limiting the victim's time with family and friends. When this is evident, you should seek advice from your medical doctor, pastor, and counselor.

2. Biblical Insight

PRAYER FOR THE ABUSED

In families who have endured a dry spell without joy, bring everlasting happiness.

When their souls feels like a desert, bring gladness and provide each flower with a safe environment of security, peace, and healing.

Like a flower, each emotion will have many blooms. It will show its happiness as if it were shouting for joy.

Let their inner selves shine through with the beauty like that of the forest of Lebanon and as beautiful as the hill of Carmel and the Plain of Sharon.

As healing is taking place, may the glory of the Lord, and the splendor of our God, illuminate their lives.

Where stress has drained their bodies of the nutrients they need to thrive and heal, place Your servants in the path of these wounded flowers, to minister to them so that You may make their weak hands strong and their weak knees steady. Build for them a firm foundation, in which they will be planted steadily in Your truths and seek Your face for wisdom and healing.

Help us to encourage those who are afraid to not be frightened, and to look to You, to place their hope in You oh God, for Your Word says that You will come and punish Your enemies. You will make them pay for the wrongs they did against us, while yet You choose to save the broken and hurting.

When they are rescued, they will see more clearly and understand more clearly that their situation was a path of despair, causing them blindness, because of how they were being treated.

Transform them in their time of healing from being emotionally, physically, and spiritually crippled, to that like a deer who will freely jump over the hurdles in their lives. Those who can't talk now will have freedom, in the name of Jesus, to shout with joy. They will share their stories so that others will be saved from the destructive hands of selfish and controlling persons and be able to give God the glory.

We praise You, Lord, for the refreshing water that will flow in their dry land of sorrow and despair.

We thank You, Lord, that the burning deserts in their souls will have pools of water to draw from. And the dry ground of their spiritual walks will have springs of living water. You will flood their lives with love, joy, peace, salvation, and security, and they will be blessed and moved with the Holy Spirit.

Place the hurting on the road to recovery and holiness. Let this road be a boundary line for the evil people, that they will not be allowed to walk on it or past it. Protect the broken by only allowing good people to walk on it, so that they will always be protected from those who seek to control and destroy their lives.

The road of recovery and holiness is only for those who God saves; the people the Lord has freed will return there, and they will enter the gates to help minister to others who are also being freed from emotionally, physically, and spiritually abusive relationships and influences.

Let their gladness and joy be contagious and overflowing, while their sorrow and sadness go far away from them. We pray Lord, that they will never turn their hearts away from You, oh God, and that You will warn, protect, and give them wisdom in times of danger. In Jesus's name we pray and ask these things, Amen.

Paraphrased from **Isaiah 35**

3. Sayings to Recite

THIS IS NOT YOUR RESPONSIBILITY

• I can **not** change or restore my abuser.

• I can **not** create an environment in my home that will **cause** my spouse to be less abusive.

• I can **not** do everything perfectly to prevent conflict. No matter how neutral I try to be, it's **never** going to make my abuser happy. I can **not** give him/her the perfect life, in the perfect environment that he/she demands.

• I can **not** promise my spouse that we will live in the perfect neighborhood with a perfect house and that he/she will have the perfect job. This life is not perfect and I am not God of the heavens who controls these things.

4. Words of Affirmation

RIGHTS OF THE ABUSED

• God has allowed conflict in my life for me to recognize that my situation needs attention and help.

• I have the freedom to tell my medical doctor that I am in a complicated and abusive situation.

• I have the right to go see a counselor.

• I have a voice. I may feel unable to verbally use it, but I can take action and walk in the direction of where help does exist.

• My abuser has stained our relationship with sin. His/her actions need to be corrected before I allow him/her to be a part of my life again.

• My abuser will continue to be abusive if I do not separate from him/her. I need to give him/her the space to better him/herself with the help of a counselor.

• I realize it may take three years or longer for my abuser to recognize his/her destructive patterns of abuse and to change from his/her dysfunctional behaviors.

• I realize that my abuser may tell me that he/she will change. I must remember that it has been proven that many abusers give up trying within the first three months of consistent treatment.

• God will change the heart of an abuser, *if my abuser is willing to work for a change.*

5. Questionnaire

RELATIONSHIP EVALUATION

Answer each question on a separate sheet of paper so you can shred the results if you need to hide your answers.

Number your paper and write down your answer to each question.

Part 1: 50 questions

Part 2: 50 questions

Part 3: 30 questions

Part 4: 40 questions

Mark each question in each of the four parts with the appropriate answer:

A-Always, S-Sometimes, N-Never

There is space at the end of Part 4 to tally your answers.

Part 1 Personal Stress-A side effect of emotional abuse.

1. I often find myself saying, "I'm sorry."

2. I can never find enough time to pursue the things I enjoy.

3. Each year I feel as if I have more stress than the year before.

4. I feel as if I am running low on energy and empty on joy.

5. It seems I am losing a lot of hair.

6. I try to stay calm and neutral at all times to avoid a tongue-lashing from my spouse.

7. I avoid my spouse when he/she is home, so I'm not a target of his/her anger.

8. My spouse only lets up from an angry speech when I succumb to his/her desires and apologize.

9. I feel as if my spouse is lacking in proving his/her love for me regularly.

10. To keep the peace with my spouse, I give him/her what he/she wants, when he/she wants it.

11. My spouse makes my family and friends feel uncomfortable when they visit our home.

12. My spouse limits the time I spend with family and friends.

13. When I am enjoying my day with family and friends, my spouse will tell me that he/she needs me to come home early or lets me know he/she's upset that I went out.

14. When I am enjoying my day with family and friends, I worry if my spouse will approve of the purchases I've made.

15. My spouse often reminds me that I need to forgive and forget past offenses.

16. My spouse willingly repeats past offenses and expects me to forgive him/her endlessly.

17. My spouse calls three or more times a day while he/she is away.

18. My spouse doesn't allow me to see the budget.

19. My spouse gives me a designated credit card to be used for approved expenses.

20. My spouse doesn't allow me to have a check card, credit card, or checkbook to our bank account.

21. My spouse allows himself/herself a budget for things

he/she wants, but I have to sneak my needs out of the grocery fund.

22. I have a secret amount of money saved up in case I need to leave my spouse.

23. When my spouse is angry, I fear he may lose control and hurt me.

24. My spouse expects me to be home when he/she gets home from work.

25. My spouse designates a time he/she wants breakfast, lunch, and dinner and becomes mad if I can't meet his/her expectations due to other obligations.

26. My spouse expects a meal made from scratch every day.

27. My spouse shares fun experiences from his/her past but my history gets pushed aside.

28. Life runs smoothly when I center our family activities around my spouse's schedule.

29. In our intimate life, my spouse focuses primarily on his/her desires.

30. I am left unsatisfied after intimacy.

31. I don't feel safe with my spouse during intimacy.

32. I feel physically exhausted.

33. I cry over family issues two or more times a month.

34. My spouse gets angry at me when I am angry or irritated.

35. My spouse refuses to take on a portion of the household responsibilities.

36. My spouse works full time and I am expected to take care of all the household responsibilities day and night, without any time off to relax.

37. Because my spouse works, I am expected to change all the diapers, handle all the bottle feedings, and do all the household chores around the clock.

38. When we move, my spouse expects me to pack most or all of the boxes.

39. My spouse punishes me by withholding my rights to drive a car, see a doctor, or work outside the home.

40. My spouse talks down to me.

41. I struggle with my self-worth.

42. My spouse gets angry when I cry.

43. When I'm having fun and something surprises me, my spouse gets angry if I squeal in delight.

44. During stressful family issues, I find comfort in food.

45. I am too busy meeting the needs of others to relax and enjoy personal hobbies and interests.

46. I struggle to comprehend reading material more than

I have in the past.

47. I struggle to follow the storyline of a movie.

48. My spouse acts inconvenienced when I get sick and when I ask to see a doctor.

49. My spouse expects me to attend activities with him/her even after I have just had a baby or when I am sick.

50. My spouse expects me to maintain all household obligations at full level, even when I am sick.

If you answered "always" or "sometimes" to more than a few answers, it's a sign that you should see a counselor. You may use your evaluation sheet as a starting point in your first counseling session, to address the issues in your relationship.

Sparks Of Discernment

Lost Purpose and Joy

When a woman is under an abusive influence, it is common to think that she can win her husband over by being a submissive wife through an excessive amount of servitude. This exacerbates the problem, enabling the abuser to refrain from seeking help. Over time, the abuser develops unreasonable expectations for his wife, and will use control as a means to have his desires met.

When a woman hits a breaking point, it's because her method of excessive servitude has failed. She becomes confused and hopeless and will likely ask, "Why has this happened?"

Victims of abuse feel as if they have lost their joy and their purpose. They take the burden of a complicated relationship upon themselves. They also manage their spouse's unreasonable expectations by controlling the emotional temperature of the home. They ignore their own rights, needs, and desires. Intervention is the only answer to the problem. A trained counselor is vital at this point. You deserve to invest in yourself and discover God's plan for you outside of meeting your spouse's needs.

Part 2 The Children

1. I'm afraid for my child's safety when my spouse disciplines them.

2. I feel as if my spouse sets unrealistic expectations for my child, that are beyond their physical or mental capabilities.

3. My spouse claims that his/her style of discipline is creative, but I question if his/her style will cause emotional distress for the children later in life.

4. My spouse pushes, trips, or runs into the child and claims that if the child hadn't been running or had watched where they were going, they would not have been hurt.

5. My spouse bullies the child with intimidation tactics to toughen him/her up.

6. My spouse teaches the child to fight and hits them to toughen them up.

7. When my spouse wants to spend time with me, he makes the child feel second class, or neglects and ignores their needs.

8. I'm uncomfortable with how much time my spouse sends our child to his/her room, the basement, or garage.

9. My spouse overreacts to mistakes made mindlessly by our child and berates him/her endlessly for it.

10. My spouse belittles the character of our child.

11. My child cries himself/herself to sleep because he/she feels like he/she will never be good enough for my spouse.

12. My spouse doesn't allow my child to have healthy friendships with other children his/her own age for more than a year or two.

13. My spouse makes unhealthy threats against my child.

14. My spouse loses control when he/she spanks or disciplines.

15. My child gets disciplined for petty offenses that weren't done out of defiance.

16. My child often acts sad.

17. When I leave my child with my spouse, he/she has unexplained cuts, bruises, burns and/or marks.

18. My child is starving when I come home.

19. My child is dirty when I come home.

20. My child is forced to beg for mercy before being let

out of a choke or restraining hold.

21. My spouse occasionally hits, smacks, or spanks my child for no reason at all, when we are at home or in public.

22. My child often cries and claims that they don't know why.

23. My child's vocabulary is unable to describe what happens to them with my spouse when I am not around.

24. My child is expected to act older than their physical age.

25. My spouse expects my child to have the mental capacity of an adult, and make better decisions because of it.

26. My child often acts angry and/or upset.

27. My child bullies other children and/or adults.

28. My child clings to me for dear life when I try to pass him/her off to my spouse.

29. My child will not look into our eyes when we talk to him/her.

30. My child is cruel to his/her toys and animals.

31. My child uses violence (hit, kick, punch) to get what he/she wants.

32. My spouse shakes or jerks my child around out of frustration or as a means of discipline.

33. My spouse pushes or smacks my child's head toward his plate, fork, or cup when he/she tries to eat.

34. My spouse becomes aggressive when he/she washes my child's hands and face after a meal.

35. My spouse gets angry and acts inconvenienced when my child cries and needs attention.

36. I try to handle all the needs of my child so my spouse doesn't lose control with him/her.

37. My spouse hits my child with a hairbrush, tool, or pan to push him/her out of the way, or to make a point.

38. My spouse sends my child to bed without food, as a means of discipline.

39. I try to shield my child from the emotional and/or physical abuse I receive, so they are not affected by what they see.

40. I intervene when my spouse interacts with or disciplines my child.

41. My spouse singles out and picks on my child until they feel worthless.

42. I feel as if my spouse doesn't like my child.

43. My spouse will not connect with my child in a positive way.

44. My spouse threatens to kill or hurt my child, to get him/her to do what is asked.

45. My child hides behind furniture or in another room because they are fearful or unsure of my spouse.

46. My spouse and/or I, yell at our child.

47. My spouse will not allow my child to express themselves emotionally (cry, be upset, share what they are thinking, express joy).

48. My spouse teaches my child that life is all work and no play.

49. My spouse expects our firstborn to lead by example and disciplines him/her more than the other children.

50. My spouse expects my child to always sit and be quiet, while the adults visit.

Sparks Of Discernment

Safety for Children

Emotional abuse is sometimes hard to define, while physical abuse is easy to pick out. A key thought for parents to ask themselves is, "Am I doing what I can to make sure my child is in a safe, stable, and happy environment?" You are the only person who sees how your family operates. Sometimes it is hard to admit when we, as parents, are wrong. Worse yet, it's hard to reach out for help, because we fear that we will lose our children to the state. We think about what is best for us, instead of what is best for the children.

The public often shows disdain and distrust for those who protect our babies in state-run facilities. However, in my personal experience as a former foster parent, and knowing those who operate within that system, I can testify to the dedication and compassion that social workers regularly invest. The ones I had during our foster care experience did everything in their power to educate each family on how to create a healthy home, emotionally and physically. Their goal is to keep the child with the parents because children thrive best with their families, once neglect and negative discipline styles have been corrected. I have had interactions with both state-run and Christian-operated organizations and they both have had the same goals in mind. My suggestion to you is to ask them for guidance in raising your family and share what your struggles are. If you don't want to go that route, seek a counselor and ask for guidance. Be open and just let your counselor know how you feel about the way that your child is being raised. Counselors, pastors, and those who protect our children all want to see the same thing: happy, safe, and confident children. We do our jobs because we love helping others find the fun in having a family, and want you to enjoy that too.

Some say the system is broken. Realize that your family is broken and there are still valuable nuggets of gold that the system is willing to offer you. There are those working in the system who can help you find and put back together those important pieces of your family as well. Always remember that if you feel you are being misled by a leader or counselor, it is important to seek a second opinion.

Part 3 Emotional Abuse

1. My spouse picks out what I am allowed to buy with my birthday money and/or gift cards.

2. My spouse holds me down against my will.

3. My spouse leaves me in dangerous places.

4. My spouse threatens to hurt me.

5. My spouse gets angry when I cry.

6. My spouse stonewalls me (cuts me off emotionally), until I submit to his/her wishes.

7. My spouse gets jealous of my gifts and talents.

8. My spouse gets angry when I win at games.

9. My spouse is jealous of my past relationships.

10. My spouse plays a lot of mind games against me.

11. Even though my spouse has never given me bruises or broken my bones, I fear that someday he/she will.

12. My spouse tries to control how much time I spend with family and friends.

13. My spouse has created a social network for me that includes all individuals in which he/she has approved.

14. I believe that I am to blame for the way my spouse

treats me.

15. My spouse sprays or throws chemicals in my face and claims that I did it to myself.

16. My spouse says I'm insane.

17. My spouse says demeaning things to me.

18. My spouse yells at me like I am a child.

19. My spouse tells me to leave, but demands that the children must stay with him/her.

20. My spouse cheats on me and tells me it is my fault.

21. My spouse doesn't acknowledge that I have the ability to make big decisions for our family too.

22. My spouse treats me like I'm a lower-class citizen.

23. My spouse acts as if I don't exist, when he/she is in the presence of members of the opposite sex.

24. My spouse makes me ask for permission before committing to a group or committee.

25. My spouse withholds the car from me.

26. My spouse sharpens/flaunts knives or other weapons to intimidate me.

27. My spouse refuses to fix the car in order to keep me housebound.

28. My spouse will threaten to hurt the kids if I don't comply

with his/her wishes.

29. My spouse screams in my face.

30. My spouse withholds affection or attention from me to punish me.

Emotional abuse changes the way you view yourself as a person. Recognizing what emotional abuse looks like is the first step in regaining your self-confidence and setting you free on a path of healing.

Part 4 Physical Abuse

1. My spouse throws things at me.

2. My spouse cuts me during intimacy and/or encourages me to reciprocate the action on him/her.

3. My spouse punches, hits, kicks, and/or pushes me.

4. My spouse uses objects to hit me with.

5. My spouse uses physical force against me.

6. My spouse puts me in a restraint.

7. My spouse shakes me.

8. My spouse binds me and hides me in a closet or some other hidden area.

9. My spouse pulls my hair, nails, ears, etc.

10. My spouse holds a weapon against me.

11. My spouse threatens to shoot, cut, burn, or drown me.

12. My spouse offers to help me with chores and then beats me up for any reason he/she can come up with.

13. My spouse bruises me.

14. My spouse breaks my bones.

15. My spouse hurts our animals and/or the children.

16. My spouse chokes me.

17. My spouse throws his/her food and/or drink and expects me to clean it up.

18. My spouse breaks my teeth, pokes my eyes, or hurts me in other ways not mentioned.

19. My spouse hurts me during intimacy.

20. My spouse does things against my will during intimacy.

21. My spouse makes me believe I am about to die and then releases me.

22. My spouse locks me out of the house or car.

23. My spouse goes ballistic and causes property damage, and then makes me clean it up.

24. My spouse beats me for calling and/or talking to other guys or girls.

25. My spouse throws hot food or beverages at me.

26. My spouse forces me to ingest or inject chemicals or drugs into my body.

27. My spouse withholds food from me.

28. My spouse expects me to be his/her slave.

29. My spouse forces intimacy when I don't feel well or before I am healed from having a baby.

30. My spouse forces me to perform for him in ways that I am uncomfortable with.

31. My spouse throws knives and/or other weapons at me.

32. My spouse forces me to be intimate with other humans or animals.

33. My spouse forces me to be a prostitute.

34. My spouse forces me to hurt myself.

35. My spouse forces me to hurt the children, animals, or other humans.

36. My spouse forces me to play Russian Roulette with a weapon or harmful substance.

37. My spouse forces me to perform in intimate ways for his/her family and/or friends.

38. I am not allowed to see a doctor after my spouse physically abuses me.

39. My spouse disciplines me the "Biblical way" by stoning me and/or by using a whip.

40. My spouse forces me to drive the car when the brakes are out and/or after the wheels have been loosened.

Physical abuse can be direct or indirect. To experience direct physical abuse is to be physically hurt by your abuser.

To experience indirect physical abuse is to be forced to watch your abuser hurt themselves, an animal, or another person. Indirect physical abuse is also a form of emotional abuse.

One or more markings for physical abuse on the evaluation sheet is not acceptable. Every woman deserves to be safe and respected. If you are experiencing or have experienced physical abuse, you can get help from your local women's abuse shelter. Evidence of physical abuse is needed. If you have a bruise, burn, or mark that proves that physical abuse has occurred, or if you have a police report confirming physical abuse, you will get the help you need.

Health Meter

Tally up the scores from each section.

Part 1 Personal Stress From Abuse

A-Almost____, S-Sometimes____, N-Never____

Part 2 The Children

A-Almost____, S-Sometimes____, N-Never____

Part 3 Emotional Abuse

A-Almost____, S-Sometimes____, N-Never____

Part 4 Physical Abuse

A-Almost____, S-Sometimes_____, N-Never____

Now combine the numbers from Parts 1-4 and place the total number in the categories below.

A-Almost____, S-Sometimes____, N-Never____

The statements in the evaluation do not cover all the different ways abuse can show up, and abuse is not limited to what you read or evaluate your relationships on from this book. Some of the statements in the evaluation are based on Power and Control Wheel Charts found on the Internet.

Your score totals are to help you come to terms with the reality of your situation. Are you in an emotionally and/or physically abusive relationship?

If you marked any of the statements, you and your spouse have some things to work on.

If you marked more than a handful of the statements, don't be alarmed at your numbers. Instead, be encouraged that it isn't over and there's still a chance for redemption. But do take action. Meet up with a pastor and a counselor to ask for alternative ways to handle the unhealthy situations that you are faced with. If your spouse is unwilling to make your home emotionally and physically safe for you and/or the kids, you may need to separate from him/her until they can prove that they are safe to live with.

Help is available. You do not have to suffer in silence.

References

Unless otherwise stated, scripture quotations are taken from the Holy Bible, New Century Version.

Mike Zannitto • Master of Science in Psychophysiology. Retired police and SWAT officer, nurse, EMT, combat veteran, Gulf War medic, Board Certified Expert in Traumatic Stress, and educator in all listed fields for over 20 years. For more information on Mr. Zannitto's important work, go to www.peacekeepersforlife.org.

IFSTA (International Fire Service Training Association) • Essentials of Fire Fighting and Fire Department Operations, 5th Edition.

Nancy L. Thomas • When Love is Not Enough: A Guide to Parenting Children with RAD-Reactive Attachment Disorder.

Dr. Robert M. Sapolsky • Why Zebras Don't Get Ulcers.

"The Great Flood of 1993" • National Weather Service, www.weather.gov, Quad Cities, IA/IL.

Stormie Omartian • The Power of a Praying Wife.

Dr. Christina Matera • "Stress & How It Affects Your Menstrual Cycle," Tampax.com/en-us/tips-and-advice/period-advice/stress-and-periods

"Stress And Periods: How Stress Affects Your Menstrual Cycle" • mellowed.com/stress-menstrual-cycle

Castings Crowns • *Lifesong*, "Father, Spirit, Jesus," "Praise You in This Storm." Beach Street Records, 2005 CD.

Dr. Tim Clinton, Dr. Chap Clark with Dr. Joshua Straub • The Quick Reference Guide to Counseling Teenagers.

Danny Huerta • www.focusonthefamily.com/parenting/cutting-is-a-call-for-help

Tim Larkin • Survive the Unthinkable: A Total Guide to Women's Self-Protection.

Tim Larkin, Chris Ranck-Buhr • How to Survive the Most Critical 5 Seconds of Your Life.

About the Author

Shelly Bronkema lives in northern Michigan, where she counsels women who have struggled from the effects of abuse. Combining the strength she has gained as a firefighter and the nurturing, attentive care she has practiced as a cosmetologist, she offers support and guidance through Under Abusive Influences Ministry (UAIM).

Since leaving her abuser, Shelly's prayer has been that the Lord would transform the abuse that she endured into fortitude, resilience, and courage that can shine as a beacon to those who are struggling to walk through their own fire.

In her time of healing, Shelly has diversified her interests, talents, and skills, and she is currently working on her Bachelor's degree in Theology. Shelly plans to combine all of her educational experiences to be used in women's ministries. Her goal is to help deepen the hearts of women so that they, too, can discover what God's purpose is for their lives on the other side of abuse. Shelly's vision is to open recovery centers for those going through the healing process of emotional abuse, providing safe havens for broken hearts, spirits, and minds to rebuild and flourish once again.

Under Abusive Influences Ministry
U.A.I.M. for Recovery After Abuse
www.uaim.info

Visit the web page to sign up for our blogs and stay up to date on how to bring recovery to your community. Share *Faith Under Fire Through Trials of Abuse* with your social media feed to reach those who are in secret about their abusive relationship.

You can find us on:

Facebook - Under Abusive Influences (@UAIMin)

Twitter - Shelly Bronkema @UAIMinistry

Instagram - counselorbronkemashelly